Skills for

STANDARD GRADE HISTORY

CW00889154

Other history titles by Philip Sauvain:

Hulton New Histories:
  1 Tribes and Tribunes
  2 Serf and Crusader
  3 Crown and Parliament
  4 Forge and Factory
  5 War and Peace
  Teacher's Book

British Economic and Social History – Book 1 1700–1870
                                        Book 2 1850–present day

The Modern World: 1914–1980

European and World History: 1815–1919

Further history titles from Stanley Thornes and Hulton include:

Kelly: *A World of Change: Britain in the Early Modern Age 1450–1700*
  World of Change Topic Books:
    A City at War: Oxford 1642–46
    Elizabeth & Akbar: Portraits of Power
    Scolding Tongues: The Persecution of 'Witches'
    Bare Ruined Choirs: The Fate of a Welsh Abbey
    Exploring Other Civilisations
    Children in Tudor England
    The Cromwell Family

Kelly: *A Place in Time: Britain 1450–1700*

Leeds: *Peace and War: A First Source Book*

Whiting (series co-ordinator): *Footprints:*
  Industry
  The Countryside
  Towns
  Churches

Archer & Shepley: *Witnessing History* (Oral history for SCE)

Whiting: *Crime and Punishment: A Study Across Time*
        (Study Book and Teacher's Resource Book)

Stanley Thornes History Series:
  Mantin & Pulley: *Investigating Sources*
  Hetherton: *Changing Britain 1815–51*
  Lankester & Mantin: *From Romanov to Gorbachev*
  Thie and Thie: *Nazi Power in Germany*
  Mantin and Pulley: *Medicine Through the Ages*

Unwin: *History for You: Britain Since 1700*

Simpson: *Changing Horizons: Britain 1914–1980*

Simpson: *Working with Sources: Case Studies in Twentieth Century History*

Skills for
STANDARD GRADE HISTORY

**PHILIP SAUVAIN
NIGEL SHEPLEY
STUART ARCHER**

STANLEY THORNES (PUBLISHERS) LTD

First published in 1990 by:
Stanley Thornes (Publishers) Ltd
Old Station Drive
Leckhampton
CHELTENHAM GL53 0DN

British Library Cataloguing in Publication Data

Sauvain, Philip *1933—*
    Skills for standard grade history
    1. Great Britain. Secondary schools. Curriculum subjects:
    History. Study techniques
    I. Title   II. Archer, Stuart   III. Shepley, Nigel
    907.1241

    ISBN 0-7487-0528-7

Cover illustration:
Watercolour of New Lanark Mills, about 1818, by John Winning. Reproduced by kind permission of The New Lanark Conservation Trust.

Typeset by Tech-Set, Gateshead, Tyne & Wear
in 10½/12½ Times
Printed and bound in Great Britain at The Bath Press, Avon.

Contents

Acknowledgements

The author and publishers are grateful to the following for supplying and giving permission to reproduce illustrative material:

Aberdeen City Library, pages 94, 122; Associated Press, pages 98, 100 (bottom), 136; BBC, page 53; Bilderdienst, page 69 (left); British Library, page 30; Bundesarchiv, page 29; City of Manchester Art Galleries, page 92; David King, page 16 (top and bottom); Edimedia, page 70; Fitzroy Collection, page 71 (right); Greater London Photograph Library, page 39; Hulton Picture Company, pages 14, 22, 61 (top), 95, 111 (right), 141; Illustrated London News, page 20; Imperial War Museum, pages 44, 114 (top); Keystone, page 27; Library of Congress, page 86; Low Estate, page 85 (top); Mail Newspapers plc, page 40; Manchester Public Library, page 48; Mansell Collection, pages 8 (top and bottom), 58, 107, 111 (left), 124; Mary Evans Picture Library, page 114 (bottom); Mitchell Library, Glasgow, page 101; Musée Royale de l'Armée, Brussels, page 115 (bottom); National Monument Record of Scotland, page 52 (bottom); Network Photographs (John Sturrock), page 88 (bottom); Novosti, pages 11, 71 (left); Popperfoto, pages 36 (top and bottom), 41, 97, 100 (top), 129, 131; Punch, pages 7 (top), 83; School of Slavonic and East European Studies, page 115 (top); Scottish National Portrait Gallery, page 87 (top and bottom); Sport and General Press Agency, page 103; Syndication International, page 72.

The photograph of Moray Place, Edinburgh (page 50), by Edwin Smith, was published in *The Making of Classical Edinburgh* (Edinburgh University Press, 1966).

The photographs of thatching on Eriskay and islanders returning to Vatersay (page 102), by Alasdair Alpin MacGregor, were published in *The Western Isles* (Robert Hale, 1949).

Introduction

HERITAGE: OUR LINKS WITH THE PAST

In 1983 *The Sunday Times* carried a report in which a journalist wrote:

> Last Tuesday I shook hands with a man who, when he was two,
> shook hands with a soldier who fought at the battle of Waterloo.
> For a moment I touched history.

Links with the past like this can be experienced every day. Your great grandmother knew people who lived at the time of the Crimean War from 1854 to 1856. You may even know people yourself who lived at the time of the First World War, from 1914 to 1918.

You can see and touch the past in the buildings and monuments near your home. Churches, castles, abbeys, mansions, houses, mills, paintings and photographs show us what buildings and people looked like in the past. Documents, books and newspapers also tell us what happened in the past. We call this *historical evidence*.

We need to know about the past in order to understand the present. Only if we find out about the history of European colonialism in Africa can we explain why the policy of apartheid was introduced and why it has isolated South Africa from the rest of the world today. Only if we know something of the history of Ireland can we begin to understand the different attitudes taken by people in Northern Ireland and the Irish Republic today.

Police marching into the Shankill Road during the 'No Home Rule' riots in Belfast in 1886

With many of the topics you study in Standard Grade history you will find a local link with the past. Blocked-up windows in an old building may remind you that many people in Britain bricked up their windows rather than pay Window Tax in the years before 1851 (when it was repealed). House, street and place names, such as Waterloo Road, Sebastopol Terrace, Ladysmith House, Palmerston Road, Nelson, and King George V Avenue, recall some of the events and personalities of the past. Statues, memorials, inn signs and house plaques may link your town directly to topics such as the Napoleonic Wars, the scramble for Africa or the Great War.

Statue of the Duke of Wellington in Edinburgh

Plaque in Bath Abbey to an eighteenth-century Governor of Bombay

This Tablet
is the last sad offering of
the purest conjugal Affection
to the memory of
RAWSON HART BODDAM Esq.
(late of Capel House, Enfield Middlesex)
interred beneath
who died at Bath on the 20th of May 1812
aged 78 Years.
In his early Youth he entered into the
Civil Service of the East India Company,
Anno Dom: 1752;
and having, through a course of the
most zealous Devotion to the Interest
of that great Body
assiduously promoted
the honor of his KING and COUNTRY,
was in testimony of
his distinguished Merits appointed
GOVERNOR of BOMBAY AD 1784,

Checklist — **The Link with the Past**

Go through this checklist when you start a new topic in Standard Grade history.

1 *Find out if there are any features, such as buildings, monuments, street names or house names near your home which link up in some way with the topic.*

2 *Which of your living relatives (if any) were alive for part of the time covered by the topic? What do they remember about this period?*

3 *What things from the past can you find in your local museum or library which link up with this topic?*

Going through the Checklist

Suppose you are studying the topic of 'The Great War from 1914 to 1918'. This is how you might go through the checklist.

1 *Find out if there are any features, such as buildings, monuments, street names or house names near your home which link up in some way with the topic.*

You will almost certainly find many war memorials in your home district. Some may depict soldiers in uniform or even weapons. You will probably be able to find out the names of the local regiments and the names of many of the local families who lost several of their members in the fighting. Often the Second World War casualties are recorded on the same memorial. You can then compare the effect of the Second World War on your community with that of the First World War.

2 *Which of your living relatives (if any) were alive for part of the time covered by the topic? What do they remember about this period?*

Your great-grandparents may be able to tell you about their experience of the First World War. Ask them if they remember the soldiers, the work done by women in the War, and whether they recall Armistice Day on 11 November 1918.

3 *What things from the past can you find in your local museum or library which link up with this topic?*

You may be able to see First World War uniforms, posters, weapons and photographs in a local museum. You will also find many books in the local library with photographs showing what trench warfare was like at that time.

EXERCISES AND ACTIVITIES

1   *Find out the dates of birth and death of your ancestors. Compile a family tree. See if you can discover what part your ancestors played in the events of the past. Did any of them serve in the armed forces? Did any of them emigrate? Were any of them immigrants from another country?*

2   *Find out which of the museums near your home has exhibits which will help you discover more about the the history of the period you are studying.*

Wedding photograph taken during the First World War

Testing Historical Evidence

WHAT IS HISTORICAL EVIDENCE?

Historians can use only a few of the many facts of history. This is why they have to select those facts they think are most important, such as the major wars, peace settlements, and treaties. These are crucial facts because they affect the relations between countries or have an effect on the lives of ordinary people.

In addition, historians also select a few of the many facts which tell us something about the lives and reactions of ordinary people at the time when these important changes were being made. Facts such as these may include a letter from a soldier who fought at Passchendaele, as a volunteer in the Spanish Civil War, or on the Normandy beaches. The letter will help us to picture what it was like to fight in a major battle. It may show us the sacrifices which ordinary people had to make. Yet it will not usually contain crucial facts. Similar examples, chosen from the hundreds of other diaries or letters from soldiers serving at the front, could serve equally well to illustrate the terrors and horrors of modern warfare.

Facts are only facts if they can be proved. We need evidence to show that they are facts and not something which a writer has made up. This means that we need to know the *source* or authority for each fact. Historians divide these historical sources into two main types.

Primary sources always date back to the actual time in the past when the event they record occurred. They are primary sources because they are based on what people saw, or heard, or created at the time. These primary sources may be in the form of words – such as a book, document, or letter. They may be in the form of an illustration, such as a painting, engraving, map, or photograph. They may also be in the shape of a building, an article of clothing, or some other relic you can touch. Some of these different types of primary source are illustrated on these pages.

Secondary sources, by contrast, are almost always in either written or pictorial form. They are usually, but not always, produced at some time (often a long time) after the event or period which they describe or portray. The writer of a secondary source, such as a history text book, may use primary sources as well as secondary sources to describe events which happened long ago.

The Daily Telegraph for Friday, 10 September 1976, announcing the death of the great Chinese leader Mao Zedong (or Mao Tse-tung as shown here).

FIGHT FOR POWER AS MAO DIES

Chinese weep in the streets

By NIGEL WADE,

The Daily Telegraph's Peking Correspondent, who is the only British newspaper staff reporter based in China.

CHINA'S 800 million people, a quarter of the world's population, have been instructed to stand to attention for three minutes a week tomorrow in mourning for Chairman Mao Tse-tung, who died yesterday aged 82.

Peking accepted with quiet sorrow the announcement of the death of the god-like symbol of the Chinese Communist revolution.

Two opposing political factions and a group of powerful military commanders must now decide who will lead the nation.

Poster dated 2 December 1919. It can be translated roughly as follows:

GERMAN WORKERS' PARTY
Munich Branch
Munich, 2 December 1919

We hereby invite you to a MEETING on Wednesday 10 December 1919, at 7.00 p.m. sharp in the large room of 'The German Empire' Inn, 143 Dachau Street (next to the Number 24 Lori Street Tram Stop).

Speaker: Herr Hitler on 'The Worst Humiliation Facing Germany'

This invitation is a ticket to the meeting. The room is heated.

The Committee
Josef Mayer
Secretary

Deutsche-Arbeiter-Partei

Ortsgruppe München

München, den 2. Dezember 1919

Wir ersuchen Sie hiermit zu der am Mittwoch 10. Dez. 1919
Abends punkt 7 Uhr im grossen Saale des Gasthauses

„ zum Deutschen Reich "

Dachauerstr. 143 (bei Haltestelle Loristr. Linie 24) stattfindenden

Versammlung

bestimmt zu erscheinen

Redner: Herr H i t l e r über

„ Deutschland vor seiner tiefsten Erniedrigung"

Die Einladung dient als Ausweis. Der Saal ist geheizt.

Der Ausschuß
I. A. Josef Mayer
I. Schriftführer
Andrästr 10/3 S.B.

THE STATUE OF FREIHEIT?

Cartoon drawn by Bernard Partridge for Punch (6 April 1938) published shortly after Hitler's soldiers had marched into Austria. 'Freiheit' means freedom or liberty. Compare this picture with a view of the real Statue of Liberty in New York.

Signatures of the two German delegates on the Treaty of Versailles, dated 28 June 1919, which brought the First World War to an end.

The Austrian Archduke Ferdinand and his wife leaving the Town Hall shortly before they were assassinated at Sarajevo on 28 June 1914. This was the act which sparked off the outbreak of the First World War.

INSTRUMENT OF ABDICATION

I, Edward the Eighth, of Great Britain, Ireland, and the British Dominions beyond the Seas, King, Emperor of India, do hereby declare My irrevocable determination to renounce the Throne for Myself and for My descendants, and My desire that effect should be given to this Instrument of Abdication immediately.

In token whereof I have hereunto set My hand this tenth day of December, nineteen hundred and thirty six, in the presence of the witnesses whose signatures are subscribed.

SIGNED AT
FORT BELVEDERE
IN THE PRESENCE
OF

The document which Edward VIII signed when giving up (abdicating) the throne in 1936.

In practice, it is sometimes difficult to say whether something is a primary source or a secondary source, unless you are given plenty of information about when, where, why, and how the source was first created. For instance, the sentence – 'The crowd listened in silence; you could have heard a pin drop' – sounds as though it might have been written at the time of the event it is describing. But it could just as easily have been written seventy years later. A picture may look as if it was drawn on the spot but it could have been drawn many years later by an artist in a studio!

Checklist — Historical Evidence

Here are some of the checkpoints you can go through when you see a historical source for the first time.

1   *Can you understand the source? What does it tell you about the past?*

2   *Does it contain abbreviations you have never come across before, references to events or people you do not understand, or words and phrases which we no longer use?*

3   *What type of evidence is it (e.g. a diary entry, a letter, an official report, a book, a cartoon, a photograph)? You can read descriptions of the main types of historical evidence you are most likely to see on pages 49–109.*

4   *Where does the source come from? Can it be trusted? (If you do not know its origin, this does not necessarily mean that the source cannot be trusted. We often get information from newspaper articles and reports written by anonymous writers.)*

5   *When was the source created? Was it created within minutes, hours, days, weeks, months, or years of the event or happening it portrays?*

6   *Is there any statement, or clue, to show that the source is actually based on the writer's own experience or on events which he or she witnessed? In other words, was the writer in a good position to say what happened?*

7   *If the source was written a long time after the event, is there any reason to doubt the accuracy of the facts recalled by the writer?*

8   *Is it a primary or a secondary historical source?*

9   *Was there any particular reason why the source was written? Was it written to please or to annoy anyone? Was it written to justify the writer's actions?*

10 *Are the facts in the source supported by facts you know about from other historical sources?*

Going through the Checklist

Here are two examples of the checklist in action. Notice how checkpoints are ignored if they do not apply to the extract in question.

SOURCE A

On Saturday the 25th Petersburg [later Leningrad] seethed in an atmosphere of extraordinary events from the morning on. The streets, even where there was no concentration of people, were a picture of extreme excitement . . . Factories were at a standstill. No trams were running. I don't remember whether any newspapers appeared that day, but in any case events had far outstripped anything the half-stifled press of the day could have conveyed to the people . . .

Near the entrance to the 'Letopis' offices, at the gates of the neighbouring factory, I met a small group of civilians, workers by the look of them.

'What do they want?' said one grim-looking fellow. 'They want bread, peace with the Germans, and equality for the Yids.'

'Right in the bull's eye,' I thought, delighted with this brilliant formulation of the programme of the great revolution.

The Russian Revolution 1917: A Personal Record by Nikolai Sukhanov, translated and edited by Joel Carmichael, Oxford 1955

Sukhanov was a socialist friend of Alexander Kerensky, the left-wing Russian leader who was later overthrown by Lenin. Sukhanov's memoirs were originally published in Russian in the Soviet Union in 1922 despite the fact that they were critical of Lenin and the Bolsheviks.

1 *Can you understand the source? What does it tell you about the past?*

It describes events in Petrograd (the name was changed from St Petersburg in 1914) on 25 February 1917 (or 10 March 1917 by our calendar). Over a quarter of a million hungry strikers, exhausted by the war against Germany, had taken to the streets of the city to protest against food shortages. The protests mounted and forced the Czar to abdicate only five days later. In April 1917 Lenin roused the crowds when he gave them the slogan 'PEACE – LAND – BREAD'.

2 *Does it contain abbreviations you have never come across before, references to events or people you do not understand, or words and phrases which we no longer use?*

Yes. 'Yid' is a highly offensive anti-Semitic slang word meaning 'Jew'. 'Formulation' means 'summary'. 'Letopis' was the name of the left-wing magazine to which Sukhanov contributed articles.

3 *What type of evidence is it (e.g. a diary entry, a letter, an official report, a book, a cartoon, a photograph)?*

It is a memoir (see page 66). A memoir is a personal description of events and people as they affected the writer. It is usually written some time afterwards – as opposed to a diary or journal written at the time.

4 *Where does the source come from? Can it be trusted?*

It is written by a left-wing Russian journalist who was an eyewitness in Petrograd at the time and who later took an important part in the 1917 Revolutions. There is no reason to doubt the accuracy of this particular anecdote.

5 *When was the source created?*

About five years after the incident – in 1922.

6 *Is there any statement, or clue, to show that the source is actually based on the writer's own experience or on events which he or she witnessed? Was the writer in a good position to say what happened?*

Yes. He describes his meeting with 'a small group of civilians, workers by the look of them' and records their conversation. As a journalist he was trained to observe and to record the things he saw.

7 *If the source was written a long time after the event is there any reason to doubt the accuracy of the facts recalled by the writer?*

He says 'I don't remember whether any newspapers appeared that day'. If anything, however, this failure to remember an insignificant detail may help to convince us that he could recall accurately the significant details in his story!

Funeral procession for the two hundred victims who died during the March Revolution 1917

8   *Is it a primary or a secondary historical source?*

It is a primary historical source, since it is based on something which the writer witnessed himself only a few years earlier.

9   *Was there any particular reason why the source was written? Was it written to please or to annoy anyone? Was it written to justify the writer's actions?*

Most memoirs are written to justify or explain the writer's actions. They are not objective. Since this particular anecdote closely mirrors the slogan adopted by Lenin — 'PEACE – LAND – BREAD' — we may speculate whether Sukhanov really 'thought' it was 'right in the bull's eye' at the time or whether he did so at a later date when Lenin made it the Bolshevik slogan. What do you think?

10 *Are the facts in the source supported by facts you know about from other historical sources?*

Only the fact that many strikers took to the streets of Petrograd on that day.

The second extract is taken from a newspaper account of the results of the Official Inquiry into the Amritsar Massacre in April 1919.

SOURCE B

General Dyer, giving evidence, said in April last he was in command of the 45th Brigade at Jullundur, and in response to a request for help from Amritsar on April 10 he sent 100 British and 200 Indian soldiers to that city . . .

During the 12th a certain number of arrests were made by the police under military protection. That evening he had a proclamation prepared warning the people against damage to property and violence, and against collecting more than four in number . . .

On the morning of the 13th [April 1919] he decided to go into the city . . . As far as he could remember he reached Jalliamwalla Bagh about 5.15. When he arrived on the scene he proceeded through the narrow entrance on to the high ground and deployed his men on the right and left. Within 30 seconds he ordered fire to be opened. The meeting was then going on and a man was addressing it. At the time of firing he estimated the crowd at 5000, but later on he heard that it was a good deal more . . . His object was to disperse the crowd, and he was going to fire until they were dispersed. The witness added 'In my view the situation at Amritsar was a serious one indeed, and communications I received from the neighbourhood were indicative of a serious rising . . . I looked upon the crowd as rebels, and I considered it was my duty to fire and fire well. There was no other course. I looked upon it as a duty, a very horrible duty.'

The *Daily Telegraph*, 15 December 1919

*This is a more correct spelling.

In fact the Jallianwala* Bagh was very confined and the crowd had difficulty in escaping through its narrow exits. Dyer did not give them a chance to escape. Instead his soldiers fired 1650 rounds of ammunition into the crowd, killing at least 379 people, and wounding over 1000 others. Six days later he issued an order forcing Indians to crawl along the ground if they wanted to use a street where a lady missionary had been attacked in an earlier incident. These actions were strongly condemned and Dyer was forced to resign from the Army three months later.

1   *Can you understand the source? What does it tell you about the past?*

It describes the Amritsar Massacre of 1919 from the point of view of the general responsible for killing nearly 400 civilians.

2   *Does it contain abbreviations you have never come across before, references to events or people you do not understand, or words and phrases which we no longer use?*

The Jallianwala Bagh was an open space in the city centre.

3   *What type of evidence is it (e.g. a diary entry, a letter, an official report, a book, a cartoon, a photograph)?*

It is a newspaper report quoting evidence given to an Official Inquiry.

4   *Where does the source come from? Can it be trusted?*

Since the journalist is describing the evidence heard by the Official Inquiry (a type of law court investigating the reasons for the massacre) we can be fairly certain that this is an accurate report of what General Dyer actually said to the Tribunal. But, obviously, it is *not necessarily* an accurate report of what actually happened on the day of the massacre. That was why the Official Inquiry was being held.

5   *When was the source created?*

Some time before 15 December 1919.

6   *Is there any statement, or clue, to show that the source is actually based on the writer's own experience or on events which he or she witnessed? Was the writer in a good position to say what happened?*

It is a direct report of the evidence given by General Dyer. The general, of course, was in the best position of all to say what happened at Amritsar. But since he was under investigation for his actions he is not necessarily a reliable witness.

7   *If the source was written a long time after the event, is there any reason to doubt the accuracy of the facts recalled by the writer?*

General Dyer was recalling events which occurred only eight months earlier, yet he was described as having said, '*As far as he could remember* he reached Jallianwala Bagh about 5.15'. You might have expected an experienced army officer to know *exactly* when he reached the scene of the place where 379 people were killed within minutes of his arrival.

8 *Is it a primary or a secondary historical source?*

It is a primary historical source, since it describes at first hand an incident which occurred only eight months earlier.

9 *Was there any particular reason why the source was written? Was it written to please or to annoy anyone? Was it written to justify the writer's actions?*

Obviously General Dyer's army career was at stake. His evidence could only be directed towards clearing his name.

10 *Are the facts in the source supported by facts you know about from other historical sources?*

Yes. General Dyer did not dispute the fact that he fired on the crowd. What was at issue was why he did it and whether or not his actions were justified.

British troops in India
in the 1920s

EXERCISES AND ACTIVITIES

1 *Use the checklist printed on page 9 to check through Source A below. Can you tell whether the writer was an eyewitness to this event or not?*

SOURCE A

In the presence of an enormous crowd of about 100 000 people lining the road for a distance of four miles [6.4 km], amid a swelling chorus of 'Long Live Gandhi!'. . . . Mr. Gandhi set out this morning to open the campaign for Independence . . .

Wealthy Hindus and impoverished labourers vied in hailing the Mahatma and as the procession slowly moved along, the crowds showered upon him coins, currency notes, flowers and saffron . . .

Daily News & Chronicle, 13 March 1930

The author of Source B (below) was an 18-year-old Londoner. On Saturday, 7 September 1940 he cycled into the countryside south of London.

SOURCE B

Weekend: 7–8 September
Pandemonium broke loose right above me. I jumped off my bike and looked up. It was the most amazing, impressive, riveting sight. Directly above me were literally hundreds of 'planes, Germans! The sky was full of them. Bombers hemmed in with fighters, like bees around their queen, like destroyers round the battleship, so came Jerry. My ears were deafened by bombs, machine-gun fire, the colossal inferno of machine after machine zooming in the blue sky ... Looking up – squadron after squadron of Spitfires and Hurricanes tore out of the blue, one by one they tore the Nazi formations into shreds. 'Planes scattered left and right, and the terrible battle came lower.

Colin Perry, *Boy in the Blitz,* Leo Cooper, 1972

2 *Look at Source B and go through the checklist on page 9.*

What famous battle was the author describing?

HAS THE EVIDENCE BEEN ALTERED?

Most of the historical evidence that you will see will probably have been altered in some way.

Almost all the extracts you read will form only a very small part of a much bigger whole, such as a small paragraph taken from a newspaper of thirty-two pages, or a few sentences from a 600-page book.

Sometimes the text of the extract may have been altered to make it easier for you to read. Extra punctuation may have been added. Old spellings may have been corrected. Words we no longer use may have had their nearest modern meanings inserted into the extract – often inside square brackets to set them apart from ordinary curved brackets.

In many cases large parts of an extract will have been left out simply because there is not enough space to include the whole of the extract in a book, on an examination paper, or in a collection of historical documents. Often the intervening words and sentences are left out because they are difficult to understand today, irrelevant, or just boring! Missing text is sometimes shown by a row of dots like this: ... This is called an ellipsis (or ellipses if more than one). It is usually impossible to tell whether the dots show that just one or two words are missing or whether they indicate that several pages have been left out. In many extracts the ellipses will not be shown, since their inclusion every time a word, phrase, sentence, or paragraph is omitted would make the text unreadable.

Omitting words, phrases, sentences, or even punctuation marks can alter the meaning of an extract.

EXERCISES AND ACTIVITIES

Many important documents and historical records have been destroyed by accident (such as in a fire) or by people who were ignorant of (or could not have known of, or suspected) their later importance. Undoubtedly some of the documents have been destroyed or altered in order to conceal the truth.

SOURCE A

Lenin, leader of the Bolsheviks during the Russian Revolution, addressing a crowd in 1920. Trotsky, in uniform, is standing beside the platform.

SOURCE B

The same scene, with alterations made by Stalin.

After the death of Lenin in 1924, there was a struggle for leadership in the Soviet Union. Trotsky and Stalin were the main contenders. By 1927, Stalin had defeated Trotsky. Stalin tried to portray himself as Lenin's most devoted follower and chosen successor.

1 *How did Stalin alter the photograph as it appears in Source A?*

2 *Why did he make the change?*

In 1953, the Conservative Prime Minister, Winston Churchill, suffered a stroke. His doctor, Lord Moran, kept a diary:

SOURCE C

June 26, 1953.

I do not like this, the thrombosis is obviously spreading. He knew that his hand was weaker, and he complained, 'I am having great difficulty in turning over in bed.' . . .

I drew up a medical bulletin:

'For a long time the Prime Minister has had no respite from his arduous duties and a disturbance of the cerebral circulation has developed, resulting in attacks of giddiness. We have therefore advised him to abandon his journey to Bermuda and to take at least a month's rest.'

Brain [a medical specialist] and I signed this. But when we had gone Rab Butler and Lord Salisbury [members of the government] altered it, and persuaded the P.M. to agree to their wording:

'The Prime Minister has had no respite for a long time from his very arduous duties and is in need of a complete rest. We have therefore advised him to abandon his journey to Bermuda and to lighten his duties for at least a month.'

They may well be right, that is of course if he comes through. For if he recovers and wants to carry on as Prime Minister, then the less we say about a stroke, the better for him.

Lord Moran, *Winston Churchill, The Struggle for Survival*, Constable, 1966, pp 410–411.

1 *Go through the checklist on page 9 (Checklist – Historical Evidence).*

2 *How did Butler and Salisbury alter the bulletin prepared by Lord Moran?*

3 *Why do you think that they made this alteration?*

4 *What political effects might the publication of the original bulletin have had?*

5 *Find an example of an ellipsis and an example of additional information in square brackets in the extract from Lord Moran's diary. How might these help or hinder your understanding of the episode?*

FACT OR OPINION?

We need no proof of some of the facts of history because we can see the events for ourselves on live television. Such an event was the treaty on reducing nuclear weapons which was signed by the American President, Ronald Reagan, and the Soviet leader, Mikhail Gorbachev, in front of hundreds of millions of television viewers throughout the world in December 1987. But facts like this, which we can witness for ourselves, are very few in comparison with those we have to take on trust from other sources.

Events in the past are historical facts because historians have evidence to prove that the events actually happened. Historians always need proof. In many ways they are like lawyers in a law court. They obtain evidence from witnesses. They examine exhibits. They argue. They reach a conclusion or verdict. In a court of law, the judge and the jury try to decide the case on the basis of the facts, not the opinions. So, too, do historians. When the members of a jury reach a decision on the basis of those facts they express an opinion themselves. Most times they are probably right. Sometimes they are wrong. So it is, too, with historians.

Sometimes it is difficult to tell if a statement is fact or opinion. If you know little about the subject you will probably have to accept the statement as fact for the moment unless it is clear that it could never be proved or disproved to everyone's satisfaction. Statements of fact are often misleading because they are not precise enough or because they contain insufficient details. For instance, if you read the following statement quickly – *'Germans worried by unemployment welcomed Hitler with open arms'* – you may accept it as a statement of fact because you do know that:

(a) many Germans were worried by the appalling problem of unemployment during the Depression years of the 1930s;
(b) many Germans voted for Hitler and the National Socialist Party in the elections of the early 1930s.

But you also know that many Germans – journalists, professors, Jews, Communists, Socialists, trade-unionists, the clergy, intellectuals, artists, etc., – were strongly opposed to Hitler. Were they *not* worried by unemployment as well?

The statement would make more sense if it was reworded – *'The Germans who welcomed Hitler with open arms were worried by unemployment'* – but even this cannot be accepted as fact. It is still an opinion, since we have no way of knowing for certain that unemployment was the key issue with the Germans who voted for Hitler. Nor can we be certain what is meant by 'welcomed Hitler with open arms'. This will mean different things to different people. Voting for Hitler at an election did not make a German a wholehearted supporter of the Nazi Party. The statement needs to be qualified. We could probably accept it as fact, if it read like this – *'Many of the Germans who voted for Hitler were worried by unemployment'.*

Checklist — **Facts and Opinions**

Use your common sense if you are asked to say whether you think part of an extract is an opinion rather than a fact. Ask yourself:

1   *Which parts of the statement can probably be proved right or wrong? A specific statement, such as the name of a person or place, a date, number, or quantity, is something which can be proved, or disproved, as a fact. Either the name, place, date, number, or quantity is correct or it is not. The same thing applies to specific events or happenings which can also be easily proved or disproved. Either they did happen or they did not. This is a question of fact and not of opinion.*

2   *Which parts of the statement are obviously opinions and not facts? You can often detect opinions where the writer uses words which have no precise meaning, such as* popular, beautiful, deeply, friendly, unpleasant, ugly, *and* unwise. *By contrast many words, such as* French-speaking, blue, fifty, *and* baker, *have factual meanings.*

Bear in mind that opinions are often very useful to a historian because they show what people felt about an issue, or an event in the past. But beware of thinking that opinions are facts simply because you agree with them!

Going through the Checklist

'A Scottish piper leading a column of marchers with their banner inscribed "From Scotland to London": a scene on the road between Aylesbury and Berkhamsted.' The Illustrated London News, 29 October 1932.

Read the following extract and then go through the checklist. The extract is taken from an article written for a daily newspaper at the time of the Great Depression in the early 1930s. Social welfare benefits were inadequate at that time. Many people were poor and hungry.

> It is difficult to recall any demonstration in Hyde Park during recent years that has touched the imagination of the onlookers more than did the march of the unemployed today. The crowd showed most interest in the men who walked with haversacks on their shoulders and boots or other oddments hanging from their haversacks, but its sympathy increased as the local men came by, men in a great many cases of poor physique, with pale, pinched faces and a look of worry in their eyes – young men with the stamp of despair on them and elderly men beside whom the hunger-marchers, chosen for their powers of endurance, looked fresh and vigorous.
>
> *Manchester Guardian*, Friday, 28 October 1932

1 *Which parts of the statement can probably be proved right or wrong?*

That there was a march of the unemployed on 27 October 1932 in front of a crowd in Hyde Park is almost certainly a fact, since it can obviously be confirmed from other sources. That some of the men carried haversacks on their shoulders with boots and other oddments hanging from them is also a factual statement. They either did or they did not. If the writer had said that the crowd 'cheered or applauded as the local men came by' we could also accept this as a fact as well. As the text is written, however, we cannot be certain that this is what he means when he says 'its sympathy increased'.

2 *Which parts of the statement are obviously opinions and not facts?*

Phrases such as 'poor physique', 'pale, pinched faces', 'fresh and vigorous', 'a look of worry in their eyes', and 'the stamp of despair on them' mean different things to different people. A supporter of the government (which had been instrumental in aggravating the problems of the unemployed) might have disagreed with these descriptions. So we have to treat them as opinions and not as facts.

Overall, of course, the opinions expressed by the writer in this extract are invaluable. They give us a vivid demonstration of the impact that the Great Depression of the early 1930s had on the unemployed. The extract (opinion) makes a far greater effect than the statistic (fact) which tells us that 2 745 000 people were unemployed in Great Britain in 1932. Nonetheless, the impression we get is one that is based on opinions rather than on facts. We have to bear in mind that writers of vivid descriptions may sometimes exaggerate in order to make their descriptions colourful and lively.

EXERCISES AND ACTIVITIES

Crowds attending the funeral of Lenin in 1924

Read through the following extracts from accounts which appeared in two British newspapers on 23 January 1924, two days after the death of Lenin (real name Vladimir Ilyitch Ulyanov), the 'Architect of the Russian Revolution'.

SOURCE A

The great leader of Bolshevism is dead . . . Lenin vanishes from the vast turmoil he has created.

Russia, resurrected from her ruins, will sit one day in judgement on his memory. For us it suffices to say that, with Lenin dead, a figure of Satanic proportions has departed from the European arena.

I well remember, and am not likely to forget, the sinister impression produced upon me by Lenin when I met him face-to-face in 1918 at the very beginning of his dictatorship . . . Although he smiled nearly all the time there was something 'macabre' in his appearance. The bloodthirsty Commissars of the Extraordinary Commission, with whom I played a dangerous game of hide-and-seek for many long months, had never been able to put the cold hand of terror round my heart as this small, shabbily dressed, uncouth looking man was able to do from the first minute he entered the room where the conference was taking place . . .

I thought to myself that surely this man, who was not afraid to dominate the [working classes] would go far on the road to a complete dictatorship of Russia. And so it happened.

The *Daily Telegraph*, 23 January 1924

SOURCE B

Lenin is dead.

Through all Russia that news has struck as the news of a deep and personal loss. For 'Ilyitch' was loved of his own Russian people – whom he understood and loved so well – as no leader of men in our time has been loved . . .

Under his dominant leadership, the Bolsheviks, because they were clearminded and resolute, took Russia from the nerveless grasp of Kerensky and his fellows . . . and started to build on the ruins of the old order the first Socialist Republic of the World . . .

His fearless honesty, his outspoken truthsaying when truthsaying was hard and unpopular; his absolute integrity; the simplicity of his private life; his deep sympathies; his mischievous sense of humour – all these won him the love of all who worked with him.

Incomparably – agree or disagree with his policies, his methods, his views – he stands out in history as the greatest spokesman, the greatest leader that the working-class movement has yet known, as one of the greatest leaders the world has known.

W.N.E. in the *Daily Herald,* 23 January 1924

1 *Use the checklist on historical evidence printed on page 8 to test each of these two sources in turn.*

2 *Which parts of Source A and Source B can probably be proved right or wrong?*

3 *Which parts of Source A and Source B are obviously opinions and not facts?*

4 *How does the account in the* Daily Telegraph *compare with the one printed in the* Daily Herald? *How are they similar? How do they differ from each other? How do you account for these differences?*

5 *Write your own newspaper account of the death of Lenin. Phrase it in such a way that it might have been equally acceptable as a news item in both the* Daily Telegraph *and the* Daily Herald *on 23 January 1924.*

ACCURACY AND RELIABILITY

Most of the extracts which you will see will be far too short for you ever to say with confidence that they are trustworthy and reliable sources of information. On the other hand you may be able to detect mistakes or inaccuracies in an extract which throw some doubt on the reliability of the historical source from which the extract is taken.

Checklist — **Accuracy and Reliability**

Ask yourself these questions.

1 *Are there any obvious mistakes or errors of fact in the extract? We can often test for mistakes by comparing one historical source with another. If there are mistakes it does not necessarily mean that the rest of the source is inaccurate. Nor does it mean that the source has no value. But it does mean that you should exercise some caution in treating the rest of the source as a reliable source of information.*

2 *Have you any reason to think that the facts quoted in the account may give an exaggerated or distorted view of the events which actually occurred?*

3 *Has the author left out any obvious facts which tell a different story from the one conveyed by the extract? Is there any reason to think that they were left out deliberately? (It may be that the author was just unaware or ignorant of these facts or could not have known about them anyway.)*

4 *Has the author used any words or phrases which show that he or she approves or disapproves of a person, an action, or an event? Does the author show any signs of being biased or prejudiced (see pages 28–34)?*

Going through the Checklist

Source A which follows is an extract from a biography of Lloyd George, first published in 1954. We can test the accuracy and reliability of this statement about the suffragettes by comparing the facts in this extract with those in newspapers published in June 1913 at the time of the incident which it describes (Sources B to F).

SOURCE A

SUFFRAGETTES

The most determined martyr of them all, Miss Emily Davidson, red-haired, green-eyed, half-demented girl, denied the sacrifice of her life when she leapt from an upper floor in Holloway Prison after a hunger-strike, was killed in the end on Derby Day, 1913, when she flung herself under the flying hooves of the King's horse as it led the field, thundering round Tattenham Corner.

Frank Owen, *Tempestuous Journey: Lloyd George His Life and Times,* Hutchinson, 1954

SOURCE B

ABOYEUR'S DERBY

At Tattenham Corner, and after rounding it, he [Aboyeur] still maintained his place [as leader of the field].

The Times, Thursday, 5 June 1913

SOURCE C

NARRATIVES OF SPECTATORS

The general impression of those who saw the incident at close quarters seemed to be that the woman had seized hold of the first horse she could reach – which happened to be the King's – not with the intention of disqualifying any particular horse, but of interfering with and, if possible, spoiling the race as a whole.

The Times, Thursday, 5 June 1913

SOURCE D

AN EYEWITNESS

They had just got round the Corner and all had passed but the King's horse, when a woman squeezed through the railings and ran out into the course. She made straight for Anmer, and made a sort of leap for the reins. I think she got hold of them, but it was impossible to say.

An eyewitness account in the *Manchester Guardian,* Thursday, 5 June 1913

SOURCE E

DEATH OF MISS DAVISON

Miss Emily Wilding Davison, the suffragist who interfered with the King's horse during the race for the Derby, died in hospital at Epsom at 4.50 yesterday afternoon.

The Times, Monday, 9 June 1913

SOURCE F

INQUEST ON EMILY WILDING DAVISON
[Tuesday, 10 June 1913]

Police-sergeant Bunn said he was about twenty yards [18 metres] away from Miss Davison when she rushed out on the course. 'I saw the woman throw her hands up in front of the horses. Some had previously passed her.'

The Coroner, in summing up, said he did not think that Miss Davison aimed at the King's horse in particular but that her intention was to upset the race. The jury would probably dismiss from their minds the idea that she intended to take her life.

The jury returned a verdict of 'Death by misadventure'.

The Suffragette, Friday, 13 June 1913

SOURCE G

Tombstone at Morpeth, Northumberland

1   *Are there any obvious mistakes or errors of fact in the extract (i.e. Source A)?*

Yes.
(a) The tombstone (Source G) shows clearly that her surname was Davison not Davidson.
(b) She died in hospital on Sunday, 8 June not on Derby Day itself – Wednesday, 4 June (Sources E and G).
(c) The King's horse (Anmer) did not lead the field at Tattenham Corner. The eventual winner, a horse called Aboyeur, was the leader (Source B).

2   *Have you any reason to think that the facts in the account may give a distorted view of the events which actually occurred?*

Yes. There is no evidence that 'she flung herself under the flying hooves of the King's horse'. Quite the contrary.
(a) Two of the sources (C and F) indicated that it was sheer accident that she was knocked down by the King's horse. In other words, she did not specifically select the King's horse in order to make her protest.
(b) Far from flinging herself *under* the horse, one eyewitness (Source D) said she made 'a sort of leap for the reins' and this was confirmed by a police officer at the inquest (Source F).

3   *Has the author left out any obvious facts which tell a different story from the one conveyed by the extract?*

Yes. The author describes her as 'The most determined martyr of them all' but fails to say that the inquest jury returned a verdict of 'Death by misadventure' (Source F).

4   *Has the author used any words or phrases which show that he or she approves or disapproves of a person, an action, or an event? Does the author show any signs of being biased or prejudiced (see pages 28–34)?*

Yes. The use of the phrase 'half-demented' is intended to suggest that Emily Davison was halfway towards being insane. This was not the verdict of the jury at the inquest (Source F). The use of adjectives such as 'red-haired' and 'green-eyed' can also be interpreted as indicating bias, since they are obviously intended to suggest that she was unbalanced, wilful, headstrong and envious of others. Nor was she a 'girl' (with its implication of inexperience and impetuousness). As you can see from her tombstone (Source G), she was a mature woman of 40 years of age.

EXERCISES AND ACTIVITIES

1   *Compare Source H (below) with Sources I, J, and K which follow.*

2   *Use the checklist on historical evidence on page 9 to examine each source first of all.*

3   *Then use the checklist on page 24 to identify any possible inaccuracies or inconsistencies in these extracts.*

On Sunday, 3 September 1939, Hitler's interpreter, Dr Paul Schmidt, took Ribbentrop's place at the German Foreign Office in Berlin to receive the ultimatum from the British ambassador, Sir Nevile Henderson, giving Germany just two hours to agree to withdraw German troops from Poland.

SOURCE H

I then took the ultimatum to the Chancellery, where everyone was anxiously awaiting me ... When I entered the next room Hitler was sitting at his desk and Ribbentrop stood by the window. Both looked up expectantly as I came in. I stopped at some distance from Hitler's desk, and then slowly translated the British Government's ultimatum. When I finished there was complete silence.

Hitler sat immobile, gazing before him. He was not at a loss, as was afterwards stated, nor did he rage as others allege. He sat completely silent and unmoving.

After an interval which seemed an age, he turned to Ribbentrop, who had remained standing by the window. 'What now?' asked Hitler with a savage look, as though implying that his Foreign Minister had misled him about England's probable reaction.

Paul Schmidt, *Hitler's Interpreter,*
edited by R.H.C. Steed, Heinemann, 1951

Hitler with Ribbentrop

SOURCE I

BERLIN
3 September

At nine o'clock this morning Sir Nevile Henderson called on the German Foreign Minister and handed him a note giving Germany until eleven o'clock to accept the British demand that Germany withdraw her troops from Poland.

William L. Shirer, *Berlin Diary,* Hamish Hamilton, 1941

SOURCE J

RIBBENTROP GIVES REPLY TO BRITISH ENVOY

Berlin, Sunday, Sept. 3 (AP) – German Foreign Minister Joachim von Ribbentrop received British Ambassador Sir Nevile Henderson at 9 a.m. today to hand him Germany's answer to the 'final warnings' of Britain and France.

The New York Times, Sunday, 3 September 1939

SOURCE K

The British declaration of war, however, took him [Hitler] by surprise. Dr Paul Schmidt, his interpreter, recorded his reaction. 'Hitler was petrified and utterly disconcerted. After a while he turned to Ribbentrop and asked "What now?".'

Brigadier Peter Young, *Wars of the 20th Century,*
Bison Books, 1985

BIAS AND PREJUDICE

Bias in history presents one side of the picture only, such as setting out only those arguments you agree with, or listing only the good or bad points (but not both). It may exaggerate or distort what someone has done or said.

An advertisement is an obvious example of bias. It does not tell you the bad points about a product. Nor does it tell you about better products from other manufacturers!

Similar bias can be found in both primary and secondary historical sources. People often gloss over, or ignore, bad points and the other side of an argument. They may select only those facts which support their case. They may use words designed to make readers feel strongly either for or against a particular point of view. Bias is often political or religious.

A historian must study evidence carefully to see if it is biased in any way. If there is bias, it does not mean the source is valueless. Far from it. The source may be valuable precisely because it reveals the attitudes of a large group of people. It shows how people felt and thought at the time.

Prejudice is an extreme form of bias. Prejudice does not listen to reason. Prejudice can be suspected if a writer is known to have, or reveals, a hatred, dislike, or an unreasonable attitude to particular people or places. This can sometimes happen, even in the writings of well-known historians. Political or religious beliefs, for instance, can sometimes lead to a very biased selection of evidence and lead the writer to a faulty conclusion. Prejudice can often be seen in writings about:

- a particular race of people (e.g. the Arabs or the Jews),
- a person – particularly one with controversial opinions, such as Karl Marx, the founder of modern communism
- the part played by women in society or in politics
- a political party (e.g. Communist, Socialist, Conservative)
- a class of people (e.g. upper, middle, or working class)
- a minority group
- a religion
- a way of life (e.g. that of the gypsies).

Anti-Semitic Nazi propaganda from 1937. How did this poster encourage the German people to be prejudiced against Jews? What does it tell us about the Nazis?

Bias and prejudice can be expressed in pictures as well, such as in pictures which caricature ethnic groups and foreigners.

You may be able to understand, or even appreciate, why there is bias – such as the bias in favour of Napoleon by a French historian and the bias in favour of Nelson or Wellington by a British historian. Nonetheless, it is still bias.

If you see or suspect bias in a historical extract you should treat the whole of the extract with caution. The writer may have allowed bias to alter the way in which certain facts are chosen and other facts left out.

When we read a newspaper, we do not often find concrete evidence that this has happened. In the following extract, however, you can see how the powerful owner of a newspaper, Lord Northcliffe ('the Chief'), tried to win support for David Lloyd George in the *Daily Mail* on 6 December 1916, at the height of the First World War. Lloyd George had just resigned from Asquith's Cabinet because he felt the war was not being fought vigorously enough.

Wednesday, December 6, 1916: Things came to a head last night and Asquith resigned. And our shout to-day across the splash page is, 'BRAVO! LLOYD GEORGE.' The King sent for Bonar Law last night. Our private information is that Lloyd George is willing to serve under anybody who is out to win the war, and that Bonar Law is his nominee for the leadership of the new Ministry. We print to-day pictures of Lloyd George and Asquith side by side. 'Get a smiling picture of Lloyd George,' said the Chief, 'and underneath it put the caption "DO IT NOW," and get the worst possible picture of Asquith and label it "WAIT AND SEE".'

He asked me what I thought of this: 'It's rather – unkind, to say the least, isn't it?' I said. 'Nothing of the sort,' he said. 'Rough methods are needed if we are not to lose this war . . . it's the only way. This Haldane gang has dragged the country into a dangerous mess.'

Other inspired headings to-day are: 'Germans Fear Lloyd George: France Wants Him: The Empire Trusts Him.'

Tom Clarke, *My Northcliffe Diary,* Victor Gollancz, 1931

BRAVO, LLOYD GEORGE!

MR. ASQUITH RESIGNS.

A TORN-UP AGREEMENT.

THE KING SENDS FOR MR. BONAR LAW.

MR. LLOYD GEORGE GETS HIS WAR COUNCIL.

COURT CIRCULAR.

BUCKINGHAM PALACE, Tuesday.

The Right Hon. H. H. Asquith had an audience of his Majesty this evening and tendered his resignation as Prime Minister and First Lord of the Treasury, which the King was graciously pleased to accept.

Mr. Asquith was received in audience of his Majesty at Buckingham Palace shortly before seven o'clock, when he tendered his resignation.

Mr. Bonar Law arrived at Buckingham Palace shortly after 9.30 in response to a summons from his Majesty. He left again at 10.10.

Mr. Bonar Law owes his position entirely to Mr. Lloyd George's action. The position of Mr. Lloyd George amid the events of yesterday and last night remains the same. He stands for a "War-Forward Movement" and is willing to serve under anybody who is "out to win the war."

Mr. Lloyd George feels that no personal considerations on his or

Prime Minister. The general opinion of our people is that they do not think the crisis ought to have arisen. The Labour Party are quite prepared to see a speeding-up of the war and are also prepared to accept a smaller War Council, but they do not think it should be arrived at by the means which have been adopted. They recognise the great driving force of Mr. Lloyd George, but they feel in a crisis of this kind the proposal to overthrow the Prime Minister is not a proper policy or one to be supported.

There is good reason to doubt whether this statement represents the opinion of the Labour Party, which consists of 35 members. The Simonites consist of a number of M.P.s who represent nobody in particular, unless the consciousness objector is to be counted as somebody.

How little the Hide-the-Truth Press understood the crisis is shown by the announcement in yesterday's *Westminster Gazette,*

tion was prompted by strong representations from his personal supporters in the Cabinet. In particular the following are stated to have persuaded Mr. Asquith to tear up the agreement of Monday:—

Viscount Grey. Mr. Harcourt.
Mr. Runciman. Lord Crewe.
Mr. McKenna.

In such circumstances Mr. Lloyd George could but offer his resignation, and he did so in writing.

Mr. Lloyd George made no overtures. He was determined not to budge au inch from the only plan, in his opinion, that will wage war successfully.

Then it was, in the language of the Hide-the-Truth Press, that Mr. Asquith "put his foot down," and

DO IT NOW.

WHAT MR. LLOYD GEORGE HAS DONE IN WAR.

Mr. Lloyd George's work during the war has two commanding qualities. The first is that he grasped the importance of time; he acted swiftly with the least possible delay. The second is that he understood the magnitude of the conflict and the stupendous difficulty of the task. While others dealt in words he was studying realities. He was indeed a force in the Government like the spring that drives the watch.

On the outbreak of war he was Chancellor of the Exchequer. He was confronted with unparalleled difficulties when Great Britain declared war on August 4, 1914. The foreign exchanges had collapsed. Credit was tottering. Prices on the Stock Exchange were falling with terrific speed. Gold was being swept out of the country.

He acted with amazing energy and decision. A moratorium was enforced to

which prided itself on being the organ through which reports of

give credit a breathing-time. A guarantee was given by the State for certain liabilities. The banking machinery

GERMANS FEAR MR. LLOYD GEORGE:

FRANCE WANTS HIM.

THE EMPIRE TRUSTS HIM.

Comment from Berlin, Paris, the Over-seas Dominions, and New York on Mr. Lloyd George's position in the Cabinet crisis can be summed up as follows:

1. The Germans fear him as the one man who means more active war upon them and prevents them from obtaining an honourable peace—i.e., a peace that will suit Germany.

2. The Allies like him as the man of action instead of words.

3. The Empire trusts him for the same reason.

4. The United States 97% of him. "He was right just as often as the others were wrong."

'RELENTLESS ANTI-GERMAN'

HUN REJOICING AT MR. LLOYD GEORGE'S "FALL."

BERNE, Tuesday.

The German Press expresses the keenest satisfaction at Mr. Lloyd George's rumoured resignation. It regards him with venomous hatred, and interprets his retirement as the downfall of the most relentless anti-German among the Allies.

The *Baierischer Kurier* says : "This is a terrible disaster for the war party in England."

The *Leipziger Tageblatt* says : " The British people have doubtless had enough of this war agitator. His fall from power brings nearer an honourable peace for England."
—Wireless Press.

From Our Special Correspondent.

AMSTERDAM, Tuesday.

ter of referendum. He considers that an assembly, however sympathetic, of twenty-three Ministers cannot reply with sufficient rapidity to the decisions of a single Hindenburg, and still less anticipate him.

In time of war the answering thrust must be immediate and the initiative instantaneous. If Mr. Lloyd George has his way Sir Edward Carson, with his brilliant qualities, will co-operate in the Ministry, and the immense naval and military war Great Britain is waging in Europe, Asia, and Africa will be effectively directed by three or four energetic, clear-headed men, who can meet and come to decisions at any hour of the day or night.

We French can only wish with complete success to the new Ministerial organisation. Our people, who are perfectly conscious of the utility of swift and strong management of affairs, will applaud all the initiatives taken by the Ententes in reply to the latest and efficacious dispositions of our enemies.

THE GREEK WARNING.

M. Stephen Pichon in the *Petit Journal* declares:

It is evidently not to weaken Britain's defences and diminish the power of her defensive that Mr. Lloyd George has acted. It is to emphasise the urgency of more energetic and better co-ordinated military, industrial, political, and diplomatic action. It is to render possible the remedying of a situation which, in his opinion, leaves much to be desired, since its distinguishing signs are the events in Roumania, the Greek rising, the unsatisfactory results on the rosters front, and the recrudescence of naval warfare which the British Admiralty has been unable to prevent.

The *Gaulois,* commenting upon the "salutary crisis" provoked by Mr. Lloyd George's action, remarks:

He has grasped, as no one in this country has grasped, how indispensable it is to the success of our military effort to entrust the conduct of the war to men of determination and competence. He has thus reached a solution of the problem that seemed in-

DO IT NOW!   WAIT AND SEE!

The Daily Mail, 6 December 1916

Checklist — **Bias and Prejudice**

Study the source carefully. If possible, compare the facts in the extract with other evidence, including engravings and photographs.

1   *Which words, phrases, and sentences seem to you to be opinions rather than facts (see pages 18–23)?*

2   *Are these opinions based on all the facts or only on certain facts which support the opinion in question?*

3   *Does anything in the extract contradict facts which you already know to be true?*

4   *Does the writer appear to take sides by presenting only one side of an argument or by showing only one side in a favourable or unfavourable light?*

5   *Is any part of the extract an obvious lie or exaggeration?*

6   *Has the writer used colourful words or phrases to try to influence the way you feel about the facts? For instance, an action may be described as being 'brave' or 'courageous' in one writer's view and 'foolhardy' or 'irresponsible' in an opposing view.*

7   *Are any of the statements controversial? This means anything with which some other people are almost certain to disagree.*

Going through the Checklist

The following extracts are taken from accounts of the show trials and purges which took place in the Soviet Union between 1936 and 1938. Thousands of senior members of the ruling Communist Party were put on trial and most were sentenced to death. They included all the members of Lenin's old Politburo (apart from Stalin), such as Zinoviev, Kamenev and Bukharin, the Red Army Chief, Marshal Tukhachevsky, and the Navy Chief, Admiral Orlov. Trotsky, the arch-enemy of Stalin, was already in exile but was hunted down and assassinated by Stalin's agents in Mexico in 1940. When the purges came to an end it was estimated that at least one million Russians had been executed and a further eight million sent to labour camps in Siberia.

SOURCE A

... in the late spring of 1936, a series of arrests of Nazi agents and Trotskyist conspirators revealed the existence of a much wider organisation – a central terrorist committee which included, not only Zinoviev and Kamenev, but several leading Trotskyists. Preliminary investigations and evidence given at their trial (in August 1936) revealed that ... the organisation was in close contact with the German Gestapo. Zinoviev, Kamenev and their associates were sentenced to be shot ...

Abroad, these trials aroused volumes of speculation, invention and abuse: abuse so sharp, indeed, that it was commonly regarded among ordinary Soviet citizens, as those who met them in these years could testify, as the most convincing proof that the Soviet Government had really struck a crushing blow at plans which had been hatched outside its borders, and that those who were responsible for the hatching were squealing.

Andrew Rothstein, *A History of the U.S.S.R.,* Penguin 1950

After Stalin died in 1953, the new First Secretary of the Communist Party, Nikita Khruschev, helped to set up a Commission to look into the purges of the 1930s. Khruschev surprised the world when he made a famous speech at a secret session of the Twentieth Party Congress in 1956.

SOURCE B

The Commission has become acquainted with a large quantity of materials in the N.K.V.D. [Secret Police] archives and with other documents and has established many facts pertaining to the fabrication of cases against Communists, to false accusations, to glaring abuses of Soviet legality – which resulted in the death of innocent people. It became apparent that many Party, Soviet and economic activists who were branded in 1937–38 as 'enemies' were actually never enemies, spies, wreckers, etc., but were always honest Communists; they were only so stigmatized and often, no longer able to bear barbaric tortures, they charged themselves (at the order of the investigative judges – falsifiers) with all kinds of grave and unlikely crimes.

Khruschev Remembers, translated by Strobe Talbott, Andre Deutsch 1971

SOURCE C

Show trial in the Soviet Union in the 1930s. The accused men are sitting on the right between the armed guards. A Soviet radio broadcast at about that time announced that 'The Trotsky-Fascist criminals who have made an attempt against the property of the Soviet State ... have deserved their merciless punishment. This is the sentence of our great country – Death to the Enemies of the People.'

SOURCE D

Later investigation established the fact that these villains [Zinoviev, Kamenev, etc.] had been engaged in espionage and in organizing acts of diversion. The full extent of the monstrous moral and political depravity of these men, their despicable villainy and treachery, concealed by hypocritical professions of loyalty to the Party, were revealed at a trial held in Moscow in 1936.

The chief instigator and ringleader of this gang of assassins and spies was Judas Trotsky. . . .

[The 1937 trials] brought to light the fact that the Trotsky-Bukharin fiends, in obedience to the wishes of their masters – the espionage services of foreign states – had set out to destroy the Party and the Soviet state . . .

These Whiteguard pigmies, whose strength was no more than that of a gnat, apparently flattered themselves that they were the masters of the country. . . .

These Whiteguard insects forgot that the real masters of the Soviet country were the Soviet people . . .

These contemptible lackeys of the fascists forgot that the Soviet people had only to move a finger, and not a trace of them would be left.

History of the Communist Party of the Soviet Union,
edited by a Commission of the Central Committee
of the Communist Party of the Soviet Union,
Foreign Languages Publishing House Moscow, 1939

Study the last source (D) carefully and then look at the way in which the checklist below has been used to test it for bias and prejudice.

1 *Which words, phrases, and sentences seem to you to be opinions rather than facts (see pages 18–23)?*

'these villains'; 'monstrous moral and political depravity'; 'despicable villainy and treachery'; 'hypocritical professions of loyalty to the Party'; 'gang of assassins and spies'; 'Judas Trotsky'; 'Trotsky-Bukharin fiends'; Whiteguard pigmies, whose strength was no more than that of a gnat'; 'Whiteguard insects'; 'contemptible lackeys of the fascists'.

2 *Are these opinions based on all the facts or only on certain facts which support the opinion in question?*

They appear to be based only on facts extorted by the Secret Police using torture (see Source B).

3 *Does anything in the extract contradict facts which you already know to be true?*

We cannot be absolutely certain that Khruschev (Source B) was telling the whole truth, since he may have been involved in the purges himself. But if his statement is substantially true, then Source D is worthless as a source of accurate information. (It is useful, however, as evidence of the hysterical attitude taken by Soviet Communists during the purges – no doubt anxious to avoid the same fate themselves.)

4 *Does the writer appear to take sides by presenting only one side of an argument or by showing one side only in a favourable or unfavourable light?*

The writer takes one side only – heaping abuse on the so-called enemies of the Soviet people.

5 *Is any part of the extract an obvious lie or exaggeration?*

Almost all of it apart from the dates and names quoted in the extract.

6 *Has the writer used colourful words or phrases to try to influence the way you feel about the facts?*

Yes, throughout – such as 'despicable villainy and treachery'; 'gang of assassins and spies'; 'Judas Trotsky'; 'fiends'; 'Whiteguard pigmies'; 'Whiteguard insects'; and 'contemptible lackeys of the fascists'.

7 *Are any of the statements controversial?*

All of them – according to Khruschev.

EXERCISES AND ACTIVITIES

1 *Examine Sources A, B, C, and D carefully with the aid of the checklist on historical evidence on page 9. Which are primary and which are secondary sources?*

2 *Go through the checklists on pages 19 and 31 with Source A. How does the author differ from the author of Source B in his account of the purges?*

3 *Which parts of Sources A, B, and D do you think are probably accurate and can be accepted as facts?*

4 *Which do you think is the worst example of bias in these extracts?*

5 *Is it possible to think of any Soviet or non-Soviet writer or historian who could give, or have given, an unbiased account of events during the purges? If not, why not?*

6 *Have you enough information to decide for yourself what really happened during the purges? What other sources might you wish to consult to confirm your opinion or to help you make a judgement?*

GAPS AND CONTRADICTIONS

As you have seen, historical sources, both primary and secondary, often contradict each other. Differences of opinion are bound to occur but sources also often disagree about the significance of important facts and events. They are sometimes inconsistent, even contradicting statements made earlier in the same document.

As you have also seen, a source will sometimes leave out inconvenient facts which do not support the opinions or claims of the writer. There may be large gaps in the records. But note that gaps in a source, such as missing days in a diary, can also occur for very simple reasons, such as absence or ill health.

Checklist — Gaps and Contradictions

Here are some of the pointers you can look out for.

1 *Does anything in the extract contradict facts which you know about from other sources? Be careful to distinguish between facts and opinions (see pages 18-23). The contradictions between sources may merely reflect different ways of looking at the same evidence.*

2 *Are there any gaps in the evidence – such as missing dates, facts, or personalities – which support a different version of the events recorded by the writer? If so, is there a good reason for this, such as illness or because these other facts were known only at a later date?*

3 *Is anything in the extract confusing? Does it contradict another part of the same document, for instance by mixing up dates, or people, or the sequence of events?*

4 *Does the writer seek to take credit for successes which other people claim for themselves? Equally, does the writer put the blame for failures on to other people?*

Going through the Checklist

Study sources A to C which are all about the London Blitz in 1940 and the corresponding British air raids on Berlin at that time. Then go through the checklist with Source C (page 37).

SOURCE A

Saturday, September 7th

Mark this day in your memory. For it has seen the opening of the first serious air attack on London . . .

There stood St Paul's with a semicircular background of red. The flames looked perilously near the dome: while to the left the pall of smoke was black – a dark pillar which drifted uneasily upward.

Anthony Weymouth, *Journal of the War Years,*
Littlebury, 1948

St Paul's Cathedral during the Blitz

Londoners using the London Underground as an air-raid shelter

SOURCE B

Towards the end of August, the Germans began to supplement their day-time efforts with fairly heavy night attacks and on 24th August a few stray bombs fell on central London. This prompted Churchill to order a retaliation on Berlin on the following night . . .

Apart from its accidental night bombing on 24th August, London was still immune from attack until the afternoon of Saturday, 7th September. I was in my office when the sirens sounded and soon both bombs and machine guns were audible. Since they did not seem to be very near I joined Winterbotham and others on the roof. Against the clear blue sky we could see, away to the east, bombs bursting and smoke billowing from fires in the London docks.

R.V. Jones, *Most Secret War,* Hamish Hamilton, 1978

SOURCE C

BERLIN

September 7

. . . the High Command said in its communiqué today: 'The enemy again attacked the German capital last night, causing some damage to persons and property as a result of his indiscriminate throwing of bombs on non-military targets in the middle of the city. The German air force, as reprisal, has therefore begun to attack London with strong forces.'

Not a hint here – and the German people do not know it – that the Germans have been dropping bombs in the very centre of London for the last two weeks.

September 11

To-day the BBC claims that the Potsdamer station was hit, but this is untrue and at least three Germans to-day who heard the BBC told me they felt a little disillusioned at the BBC radio's lack of veracity [accuracy or honesty]. The point is that it is bad propaganda for the British to broadcast in German to the people here that a main station has been set on fire when it hasn't been touched . . .

William L. Shirer, *Berlin Diary,* Hamish Hamilton 1941
(Shirer was an American journalist
in Berlin between 1934 and 1940.)

1   *Does anything in the extract contradict facts which you know about from the other sources?*

Yes. On 7 September the author says that the Germans have not admitted that they 'have been dropping bombs in the very centre of London for the last two weeks'. This is contradicted by Source A. Anthony Weymouth said that 7 September marked the 'opening of the first serious air attack on London'. Source B confirms this, 'Apart from its accidental night bombing on 24th August, London was still immune from attack until the afternoon of Saturday 7th September.' The reason for the discrepancy, of course, was that Shirer was in Berlin, not London.

2 *Are there any gaps in the evidence – such as missing dates, facts, or personalities – which support a different version of the events recorded by the writer?*

Not so far as we can tell but in wartime all contestants censor information and spread lies about their opponents. Gaps and contradictions are only to be expected.

3 *Is anything in the extract confusing? Does it contradict another part of the same document, for instance by mixing up dates, or people, or the sequence of events?*

No – apart from the question of the raids on London.

4 *Does the writer seek to take credit for successes which other people claim for themselves? Equally, does the writer put the blame for failures on to other people?*

This checkpoint is usually only of relevance in cases where the writer is a participant (like Churchill) rather than an observer (like Shirer).

EXERCISES AND ACTIVITIES

1 *Go through the checklist on page 35 with the other sources (D to K) below. Compare them with Sources A to C. What inconsistencies are there between these different sources?*

2 *What important gap was there in H.C. Knickerbocker's account of the London Blitz which he was going to write for American readers (Source E)? Why was there such a gap? When was this news released to people in Britain?*

3 *What examples of propaganda or misleading information are illustrated in Sources A to K?*

SOURCE D

Weekend: 7–8 September
A special News came over the radio at 10.15 this morning [Sunday], regarding the casualties and damage of the raids. 400 people, at least, were killed in these few hours of air-attacks. It is estimated 1,300–1,400 are seriously injured . . . London's Dockland is on fire. Houses galore in the East End are no more.

16 September
We shot down 189 'planes yesterday. We only lost 25 fighters. Magnificent.

Colin Perry, *Boy in the Blitz,* Leo Cooper, 1972

SOURCE E

12th September, 1940
Knickerbocker [an American journalist] dashes up to me aflame with rage. He says he has the best story in the world and the censors are holding it up. It is the story about the time-bomb outside St Paul's Cathedral which may go off at any moment and destroy the great work of Sir Christopher Wren. 'Cannot the American people be brought in to share my anxiety?' Also why is he not allowed to mention the destruction of Bond Street and the Burlington Arcade, so dear to many Americans?

Harold Nicolson, *Diaries and Letters 1939–1945,*
Collins, 1967

SOURCE F

8.0 p.m., Sunday 15 September
John Martin, my Principal Private Secretary, came in with the evening budget of news from all over the world. It was repellent. 'However,' said Martin, as he finished this account, 'all is redeemed by the air. We have shot down one hundred and eighty-three for a loss of under forty.' Although post-war information has shown that the enemy's losses on this day were only fifty-six, September 15 was the crux of the Battle of Britain.

Sir Winston Churchill, *The Second World War:
Volume 2: Their Finest Hour,* Cassell, 1949

SOURCE G

Sunday, September 15th
... we brought down 186 German planes today, for the loss of thirteen pilots, and it looks as if Hitler cannot keep up this pressure for long.

John Colville

London bomb damage

SOURCE H

16 September
Yesterday's battle was immense, with 187 brought down for a loss
of no more than 25 British planes and about 12 pilots.
                    General Raymond E. Lee (US military attaché in London)

SOURCE I

Monday, 16 September
Cabinet in War Room at 12. Not quite so gloomy. Wonderful day
in the air yesterday – 185 to 25 (11 pilots safe). Also damage reports
not so alarming.

                                                    Sir Alexander Cadogan

SOURCE J

GREATEST DAY FOR RAF

Half Raiders Brought Down

26 FT. DOWN

They Battled with Ton Time-bomb

350 CAME, ONLY 175 RETURNED

HITLER'S air force returned to mass daylight raids yesterday and the R.A.F. gave them the most shattering defeat they have ever known.

The Air Ministry state that between 350 and 400 enemy aircraft were launched in two waves against London and south-east England.

Of these no fewer than 175 were shot down, four of them by A.A. fire. This is a proportion of nearly one in two destroyed. All these are "certainties," for the total does not include "probables."

The R.A.F. lost 30 'planes, and ten of the pilots are safe.

Most of the raiders that were not destroyed were harassed all the way back to France.

A considerable section of Hitler's invasion fleet in the Channel ports have now been destroyed by the R.A.F.

On Saturday night our bombers gave the invasion ports their most severe battering to date.—See Back Page.

Another Hospital Bombed

PATIENTS SAFE

By Daily Mail Raid Reporter

GERMAN bombers, bound on their nightly terror raiding, arrived at 8.10 last evening.

London's terrific barrage of A.A. guns, stronger than ever at times, forced them to adopt new tactics.

WEST DOOR

THIS Daily Mail picture-diagram shows the task that faced the St. Paul's bomb squad. You can see the direction in which the bomb was slipping, 25ft. down, threatening the Cathedral more and more each moment.

ST. PAUL'S IS SAVED BY SIX HEROES

By Daily Mail Reporter

A LITTLE party of experts—an officer, Lieut. R. Davies and five men—have saved St. Paul's Cathedral from almost certain destruction by a gigantic German time-bomb which fell from a 'plane on Thursday and buried itself 26ft. deep in a crater near the walls.

Yesterday at noon, after three days' continuous work, the bomb, 8ft. long, fitted with fuses which made it perilous to handle, was secured by steel tackle and hauled to the surface with a pulley and cable attached to two lorries.

It was one of the biggest that had fallen in London and weighed a ton.

A City fireman who had been on duty continuously in the area told me:

"There were five of them, all young fellows, officered by a French-Canadian. One was an Irishman and a couple came from Yorkshire. Another, I believe, came from Lancashire.

"On the first day they couldn't start work because a six-inch gas-main, broken by the bomb, was blazing. But they've been here from early morning till dusk ever since.

Westminster Abbey Hit

The west window of Westminster Abbey was slightly damaged during a recent air-raid.

"The damage was very slight, and only a few small squares were broken," said an official.

Headlines in the Daily Mail, Monday, 16 September 1940

SOURCE K

It was hours before Fighter Command knew the extent of their
losses – twenty-six planes, thirteen pilots – though the legend of
their counter-claim was to persist for many years: a total bag of 183
German planes. Within days, Air Ministry crash investigators had
arrived at the truth: the German losses totalled no more than fifty-
six, of which thirty-four were bombers.

                                    Richard Collier, *1940 The World In Flames,*
                                                    Hamish Hamilton, 1979

EYEWITNESSES AND HEARSAY EVIDENCE

The assassination of President Kennedy at Dallas, Texas, on 22 November 1963. The President has slumped down in his seat and leans towards his wife Jacqueline Kennedy. When you look at a photograph like this you become an eyewitness yourself to one of the dark moments of history.

Eyewitness evidence can take many different forms. A newspaper report, a broadcast, a diary, a photograph, a letter, a television news report, a newsreel film, and a drawing are just some of the different ways in which eyewitnesses have recorded the things they have actually seen or heard. In other words they have witnessed an event or happening with their own eyes and ears. Hence 'eyewitness'. Eyewitnesses can be mistaken but their evidence must be taken seriously if they were really in a position to see or hear something significant.

In a court of law, the evidence from an eyewitness is carefully examined by a judge and by lawyers. It is their job to test the reliability of the witness. They try to make sure that the evidence given is truthful, exact, and accurate. They test the witness to make sure that he or she was not mistaken.

In many cases we cannot question the eyewitnesses who tell us what happened in the past. But we can compare their evidence with other eyewitness accounts and with facts we know about from other sources. We can also use common sense. For instance, how likely is it that someone will have been able to remember the exact words of a conversation which took place fifty years earlier? We ask questions to test the reliability of the evidence to see if the eyewitnesses can really be believed. Was the eyewitness in a good position to see what happened?

Sometimes a source may give the impression that the writer was an eyewitness when in fact the evidence is really based on a report of the incident which the writer heard from someone else. This is called *hearsay evidence.* Witnesses are not usually allowed to use hearsay evidence in a court of law, since there may be no way of checking whether it is accurate.

Hearsay evidence is sometimes used by historians, however, with some reservations. This is because it may have been altered or misunderstood by the person who heard it in the first place. Nonetheless, hearsay evidence is often the only way we have of knowing what went on at a private or secret meeting. For example, you might see something like this in the memoirs of Green:

> I had a long conversation with Black on the 10th. She told me that Brown had stormed out of the Cabinet in a temper.

In other words, Black was the eyewitness *not* Green (i.e. assuming that Black was herself at the Cabinet meeting in question). It would be eyewitness evidence only if Green had been at the Cabinet meeting herself. Instead, it is hearsay evidence and accordingly cannot be entirely trusted since Black could have heard the report from White and White could have heard it from Grey! We have no way of knowing for certain unless the report is backed up by evidence from other sources.

A particular problem with eyewitnesses is the question of when they put their recollections down on paper for the first time or in some other permanent form.

Although eyewitness evidence has many advantages there is a danger in thinking that an eyewitness must know the truth, or that an eyewitness would not tell a lie. In fact, many eyewitnesses see only a small part of what actually happens. Their evidence is just as liable to bias or distortion as that of writers who were not on the scene at the time of the event.

Checklist — **Evidence from Eyewitnesses**

1   *Does the source indicate in any way that the eyewitness actually saw or experienced the events recorded? We can often find this out from the evidence itself. Look out for clues in the writing which suggest that the writer was actually present, such as the use of 'I' and 'me' – as in 'I saw', 'I heard', 'a woman next to me', 'I tripped and fell'. Other statements may strongly suggest that the writer was an eyewitness, although they could have come from other sources, such as 'the crowd gasped', 'the smell was overpowering'.*

2   *Does the source indicate in any way that it is wholly or partly based on hearsay evidence?*

3 Is there any clue to show that the eyewitness was in a good position to see what happened?

4 Does the evidence justify the actions of the eyewitness in any way? This does not mean that the evidence cannot be trusted, but it does show that the eyewitness is not impartial.

5 Are there any other reasons why we may need to treat the evidence of the eyewitness with caution?

6 Is there any way of confirming any of the facts described by the eyewitness?

Going through the Checklist

SOURCE A

THE BATTLE OF EL ALAMEIN
23rd October [1942]

The whole area is now thick with vehicles of various units trying to find their designated locations. A cold wind is blowing in from the sea. I feel rather nervous waiting about in the open – our barrage is due at twenty to ten and then the form will be pretty keen ...

Right on time the barrage bursts, the whole line leaps into life. According to griff [information], it's a record effort: 800 guns of all calibres along the whole Front, one gun every dozen yards, each gun with hundreds of shells. It's certainly a rousing display. The guns nearby crash incessantly, one against another, searing the darkness with gashes of flame, and those farther up and down the line rumble wrathfully and convulse the northern and southern horizons with ceaseless flashing and flickering. Groups of Jock infantry, in shorts and shirts and tin-hats, with bayonets fixed, begin filtering forward through the gap. Poor devils – I don't envy them their night's work. ...

[later the same night]
I get down in the trench also for a spot of kip, while the sergeant minds the phone. But it's hard to sleep. The guns are still bashing away, and now the planes are going over, so that the whole sky is resonant with throbbing and droning. I look straight up into the face of the moon, which is waxen and pallid and wears an expression, so it seems to me, of incredulous dismay at the fantastic scene being enacted down here on this patch of earth.

The Battle of El Alamein

24th October
When the sergeant gently wakes me by the shoulder it's first light, eerily quiet ...

The sergeant tells me the latest news. ... The Jocks have apparently gained all their objectives, and so far there's been no sign of any counter-attack.

Feel a bit more cheerful after a brew and cigarette, and when the sun appears ...

I don't like this place. It's more uncomfortably crowded than ever this morning. Behind us the whole visible desert is cluttered with vehicles, with only a few yards between each, and still more batches coming in. We glare ferociously whenever any newcomers threaten to park too near our trench. What a target for enemy guns, or the Luftwaffe!

R.L. Crimp, *The Diary of a Desert Rat,*
edited by Alex Bowlby, Leo Cooper, 1971

1   *Does the source indicate in any way that the eyewitness actually saw or experienced the events recorded?*

Yes – 'I feel rather nervous waiting about in the open ...'

2 *Does the source indicate in any way that it is wholly or partly based on hearsay evidence?*

One sentence only is based on hearsay evidence – 'The sergeant tells me the latest news ... The Jocks have apparently gained all their objectives, and so far there's been no sign of any counter-attack.'

3 *Is there any clue to show that the eyewitness was in a good position to see what happened?*

Yes – 'Behind us the whole visible desert is cluttered with vehicles ...'

4 *Does the evidence justify the actions of the eyewitness in any way?*

No. There are no heroics. For instance, the author is not afraid to say he is 'nervous waiting about in the open'.

5 *Are there any reasons why we may need to treat the evidence of the eyewitness with caution.*

No.

6 *Is there any way of confirming any of the facts described by the eyewitness?*

Only in general – by comparing this account with other descriptions of the start of the battle of El Alamein.

SOURCE B

HAMBURG, 25 July 1943

Back in our flat we stand on the balcony and see nothing but a circle of flames around the Alster, fire everywhere in our neighbourhood. Thick clouds of smoke are hanging over the city, and smoke comes in through all the windows carrying large flakes of fluttering ash ...

There is no proper daylight the following morning, the town is so shrouded in smoke. The sun cannot fight its way through, but looks like a bloodshot eye on to the devastation. It remains like that all through the day; the smell of burning is all-pervading, so are the dust and the ash. And the siren never stops. Maria is in such a state that every time it sounds she makes a dash for the cellar with flying hair and apron strings, and we do not get anything to eat until 5 o'clock after another very heavy day raid, which was worse for the Hahns than for us. Jacoba told us about it afterwards. They cowered in the cellar, Fritz between them, holding a big cushion over his little blond head. The noise was so colossal, and everything shook and trembled so, that they made up their minds there and then: we must get away at once! She telephoned in the evening and told me of their decision; I still thought they were exaggerating and tried to calm her.

Mathilde Wolff-Monckeberg, *On the Other Side,*
translated and edited by Ruth Evans, Peter Owen, 1979

Bomb damage in Hamburg

1 *Does the source indicate in any way that the eyewitness actually saw or experienced the events recorded?*

Yes – 'Back in our flat we stand on the balcony and see nothing but a circle of flames around the Alster . . .'

2 *Does the source indicate in any way that it is wholly or partly based on hearsay evidence?*

Partly – the section which begins 'Jacoba told us about it afterwards. They cowered in the cellar, Fritz between them . . .' is hearsay evidence – since the writer heard about it from Jacoba. She did not witness it directly herself.

3 *Is there any clue to show that the eyewitness was in a good position to see what happened?*

Yes – 'we stand on the balcony and see nothing but a circle of flames . . .'

4 *Does the evidence justify the actions of the eyewitness in any way?*

No.

5 *Are there any reasons why we may need to treat the evidence of the eyewitness with caution?*

No.

6 *Is there any way of confirming any of the facts described by the eyewitness?*

Only by comparing this account with similar descriptions of the same air raid from similar sources.

EXERCISES AND ACTIVITIES

The following extract is taken from an account of the Peterloo Massacre in 1819. It was written by Samuel Bamford, a Lancashire cotton weaver who was a reformer, a radical, and a political agitator at that time. He wrote the book from which this extract is taken in 1839–42.

Bamford estimated that about 80 000 people assembled at St Peter's Field in Manchester on Monday, 16 August 1819. Most were workers in the local textile industries. Their purpose was to demonstrate in favour of Parliamentary Reform. At that time only a small handful of people, most of them wealthy, were able to vote at elections. Manchester, a large industrial city, was not even represented in Parliament. The organisers of the demonstration, such as Samuel Bamford, wanted the demonstration to be peaceful and law-abiding in order to impress the authorities. He said, 'I hoped their conduct would be marked by a steadiness and seriousness befitting the occasion.'

The meeting was addressed by a fiery Radical speaker called Henry 'Orator' Hunt. Soon after he began to speak, Bamford, who was on the edge of the crowd, heard 'a noise and strange murmur'. Standing on tiptoe, he saw the cavalry 'come trotting sword in hand, round the corner'.

On the cavalry drawing up they were received with a shout, of good will, as I understood it. They shouted again, waving their sabres over their heads; and then, slackening rein, and striking spur into their steeds, they dashed forward, and began cutting the people.

'Stand fast,' I said, 'they are riding upon us, stand fast.' And there was a general cry in our quarter of 'Stand fast.' The cavalry were in confusion: they evidently could not, with all the weight of man and horse, penetrate that compact mass of human beings; and their sabres were plied to hew a way through naked held-up hands, and defenceless heads; and then chopped limbs, and wound-gaping skulls were seen; and groans and cries were mingled with the din of that horrid confusion. 'Ah! ah!' 'for shame! for shame!' was shouted. Then, 'Break! break! they are killing them in front, and they cannot get away'; and there was a general cry of 'break! break!' For a moment the crowd held back as in a pause; then was a rush, heavy and resistless as a headlong sea; and a sound like low thunder, with screams, prayers, and imprecations from the crowd-moiled, and sabre-doomed, who could not escape.

Samuel Bamford, *Passages in the Life of a Radical*,
written between 1839 and 1842, and first published in 1844

1 *If 'turmoil' means 'confusion' what do you think 'crowd-moiled' means? What did Bamford mean by 'sabre-doomed'?*

2 *Go through the extract using the checklists for historical evidence on page 9 and for eyewitness evidence on pages 42 and 43.*

3 *Is it likely that anyone caught up in the crowd on that day would ever forget it? What importance should be given to the fact that Bamford wrote his account in 1839-42, not 1819?*

4 *Compare Bamford's account of the Peterloo Massacre with other eyewitness accounts, for instance those printed on pages 237–40 of Philip Sauvain,* British Economic and Social History: 1700–1870 *(Stanley Thornes, 1987).*

Who were the 'Manchester Heroes' in this cartoon?

Different Types of Historical Evidence

RELICS FROM THE PAST

Some of the relics from the past which we can see and touch are called *archaeological remains*. Archaeology is the science which studies the past through the materials left behind by people in the past. Much of what we know from archaeology has been discovered by unearthing pottery, tools, bones, and the remains of buildings buried in the ground. Thirty years ago people thought of archaeology as being concerned only with prehistory – the period before there were written documents to tell us about past events and past peoples. This has changed. Nowadays archaeologists study the recent past as well as the distant past. Industrial archaeology, in particular, is concerned with the tools, machines, engines, mills, and early factories which marked the beginnings of the Industrial and Agricultural Revolutions.

Checklist — **Relics from the Past**

Studying the past at a site such as a battlefield, or in a museum, or from photographs can be a very useful way of backing up what you know from other historical sources, like documents. If you do make such a study, this checklist may be useful in helping you to find out more about the subject.

1   *What was the purpose of the tool, machine, vehicle or building you are studying? What was it used for? Why was it built or made?*

2   *Can you date the object or building either exactly or approximately?*

3   *Where is it situated now or where was it found? Where did it come from originally?*

4   *What does it tell us about people in the past?*

Going through the Checklist

Part of Moray Place, Edinburgh

1 *What was the purpose of the object or building you are studying? What was it used for? Why was it built or made?*

Moray Place is part of Edinburgh's New Town, which was built to provide houses for the wealthier citizens when the Old Town had become too overcrowded, dirty and unfashionable.

2 *Can you date the object or building either exactly or approximately?*

Yes – approximately. The style of building has many typically Georgian features, such as the classical columns and the pediment. So it was probably built in the late eighteenth or early nineteenth century.

We would need to find documentary evidence to discover the precise date. This would show that Moray Place was built in the 1820s. The historian Lord Macaulay wrote in 1828 that it was 'equal to the houses in Grosvenor Square – superior to any in Portman Square that I have seen.'

3 *Where is it situated now or where was it found? Where did it come from originally?*

This is a photograph of part of Moray Place, taken in Edinburgh a few years ago. Although the layout of the site and the original Georgian architecture of the 1820s have been largely preserved, it is apparent from any visit to Moray Place that there have been changes. Few people today can afford such large houses, so they have been converted into flats and offices.

4 *What does it tell us about people in the past?*

It tells us about the grandeur of the life of Edinburgh's upper class in the early nineteenth century, and their taste for the classical style of Georgian architecture. These spacious and elegant houses might be contrasted with the squalid and cramped tenements of the Old Town where the poor lived.

EXERCISES AND ACTIVITIES

Look at the relics from the past shown in the photographs on the next page. Go through the checklist with each one and see what you can deduce from the photographs. Are there relics like these in your town?

Gas lamp in London's West End

Boot scrapers outside the door of a Georgian house in Saffron Walden in Essex

A mortsafe in an Edinburgh graveyard

DOCUMENTARY EVIDENCE

Anything that is written down (such as a letter), or printed (such as a newspaper) is called *documentary evidence*. It includes wills, Acts of Parliament, advertisements, posters, timetables, receipts, letters, journals, diaries, and anything else in written or printed form.

```
                              Sunday,
                              7th December, 1941.
                              Midnight.


        Here is the News, and this is Alvar Lidell reading it.

        Japan's long-threatened aggression in the Far East began

   tonight with air attacks on United States naval bases in the

   Pacific.   Fresh reports are coming in every minute; and the latest

   facts of the situation are these:-

        The Japanese air raids were made on the Hawaiian islands

   and the Philippines;  observers' reports say that an American

   battleship has been hit, and that a number of the Japanese bombers

   have been shot down.   A naval action is in progress off Honolulu;

   an American transport with timber on board has been torpedoed in

   the Pacific, and another cargo ship is reported in distress.

   President Roosevelt has told the Army and Navy to act on their

   secret orders, has called a meeting of Ministers, and is preparing

   a report for Congress.   In London, Mr. Winant has seen Mr.Churchill,

   and both Houses of Parliament have been summoned for tomorrow

   afternoon to hear a statement on the situation.   Messages

   from Tokio say that Japan has announced a formal declaration of war

   against both the United States and Britain.
```

The script of the BBC news bulletin announcing the Japanese attack on Pearl Harbor in 1941

The first thing you should do when you see documentary evidence like this is to read it through carefully to make sure you understand what it means. Then examine it closely to see how far you can trust it as a reliable piece of historical evidence. You can do this with the aid of the master checklist which follows. As you can see, it combines the earlier checklists printed on pages 9 (historical evidence), 19 (facts and opinions), 24 (accuracy and reliability), 31 (bias and prejudice), 35 (gaps and contradictions) and 42–43 (eyewitnesses). It is also printed at the back of the book on page 143 as a convenient source of reference. When you use this master checklist, ignore checkpoints which are irrelevant to the extract you are studying or for which you have insufficient information to make a sensible response.

Master Checklist — **Documentary Evidence**

1 *What does the source tell you about the past?*

2 *What is the origin of the source? What type of evidence is it (e.g. diary, letter, newspaper report)? Is it likely to be reliable?*

3 *Why was the source written? Was it written to justify the writer's actions? Does the writer try to take credit for successes which other people claim for themselves? Does the writer put the blame for failures on to other people?*

4 *When was the source written? Is it a primary source dating from the time of the event which it describes? Or is it a secondary source?*

5 *Is there any clue or statement to show that it is an actual eyewitness account? Was the writer in a good position to say what happened? Does the source agree with other eyewitness accounts of the same event? Are there any reasons for thinking the eyewitness cannot be trusted entirely?*

6 *If the source was written years after the event, is there any reason to doubt the accuracy of the writer's memory?*

7 *Which parts of the extract seem to you to be opinions and not facts which can be proved right or wrong? Are the opinions based on facts or on prejudice? Has the writer used words of approval or disapproval, or colourful or exaggerated phrases, to try to influence the reader?*

8 *Does the author show any other signs of bias or prejudice? Does the writer appear to take sides in an argument?*

9 *Are there any obvious mistakes or errors of fact in the extract? Which statements are supported by facts you know about from other sources? Does anything in the extract contradict other sources, or facts which you already know to be true?*

10 *Does the account give a distorted view of events which actually occurred? Has the author left out facts which tell a different story? Is any part of the extract an obvious lie or exaggeration? Are there any obvious gaps in the evidence, such as missing dates, facts, or personalities?*

Going through the Checklist

Here is an example of the way in which the master checklist can be used to evaluate a historical source. It describes a private meeting in Munich between the British prime minister, Neville Chamberlain, and the German dictator, Adolf Hitler, at the time of the signing of the Munich Agreement in 1938.

SOURCE A

Letter from Neville Chamberlain (British prime minister)
to his two sisters: 2 October 1938

I asked Hitler about 1 in the morning [on 30 September], while we were waiting for the draftsmen, whether he would care to see me for another talk. He jumped at the idea, and asked me to come to his private flat, in a tenement house where the other floors are occupied by ordinary citizens. I had a very friendly and pleasant talk: on Spain (where he too said he had never had any territorial ambitions), economic relations with SE Europe, and disarmament. I did not mention colonies, nor did he. At the end I pulled out the declaration, which I had prepared beforehand, and asked if he would sign it. As the interpreter translated the words into German, Hitler frequently ejaculated *'Ja, Ja,'* and at the end he said 'Yes, I will certainly sign it; when shall we do it?' I said 'Now', and we went at once to the writing-table, and put our signatures to the two copies which I had brought with me.

K. Feiling, *The Life of Neville Chamberlain*,
Macmillan, 1946

1 *What does the source tell you about the past?*

It explains the circumstances which enabled Neville Chamberlain to get Hitler to sign the notorious document (Source B) which asserted 'the desire of our two peoples never to go to war with one another again'. On 1 October 1938, Chamberlain said of this document, 'I believe it is peace for our time'. Eleven months later he declared war on Germany.

2 *What is the origin of the source? What type of evidence is it (e.g. diary, letter, newspaper report)? Is it likely to be reliable?*

It is a private letter, from the British prime minister to his two sisters, giving a personal account of his private meeting with Hitler. At first sight it looks as if it must be the only authoritative source of information in English of what actually happened, since Hitler left no documents to confirm or deny Chamberlain's account of the meeting. However, there was someone else present at that meeting – 'the interpreter' who 'translated the words into German'. Hitler's interpreter was Dr Paul Schmidt and he later wrote his own account of this meeting (Source C below). As you will see it does not confirm Chamberlain's impression of 'a very friendly and pleasant talk'.

3 *Why was the source written? Was it written to justify the writer's actions? Does the writer try to take credit for successes which other people claim for themselves? Does the writer put the blame for failures on to other people?*

It justifies – or, at least, explains – the actions of the British prime minister, since they were, and still are, a matter of great controversy.

4 *When was the source written? Is it a primary source dating from the time of the event which it describes? Or is it a secondary source?*

It was written only two days after the event, so it is a primary source.

5 *Is there any clue or statement to show that it is an actual eyewitness account? Was the writer in a good position to say what happened?*

It is obviously an actual eyewitness account. The writer was in a good position to say what happened at the meeting. But he did not speak German fluently enough to speak directly to Hitler. Consequently the interpreter, who spoke both English and German, was in an even better position to say what happened (Source C).

6 *If the source was written years after the event is there any reason to doubt the accuracy of the writer's memory?*

This checkpoint does not apply since it was written only two days after the meeting.

7 *Which parts of the extract seem to you to be opinions and not facts which can be proved right or wrong?*

   (a) That Hitler 'jumped at the idea' of signing the celebrated peace declaration.
   (b) That Chamberlain and Hitler 'had a very friendly and pleasant talk'.

8 *Does the author show any other signs of bias or prejudice? Does the writer appear to take sides in an argument?*

No.

9 *Are there any obvious mistakes or errors of fact in the extract? Which statements are supported by facts you know about from other sources? Does anything in the extract contradict other sources, or facts which you already know to be true?*

No. The fact that the meeting took place in Hitler's house, the general topics of conversation, and the circumstances surrounding the signing of the 'piece of paper' are confirmed by Dr Paul Schmidt (Hitler's interpreter) in Source C (below).

10 *Does the account give a distorted view of events which actually occurred?*

Not as far as we can tell from the extract on its own. But Chamberlain took a much more optimistic view of Hitler's attitude than Hitler's own interpreter did (see Source C below). Dr Paul Schmidt thought that Hitler looked 'pale and moody' and that he only 'listened absent-mindedly' to Chamberlain and contributed 'little to the conversation'. The interpreter did not agree that Hitler was keen to sign the declaration. 'My own feeling was that he agreed to the wording with a certain reluctance and I believe he appended his signature only to please Chamberlain.' Bear in mind, of course, that these are differences of opinion, and not differences of fact.

SOURCE B

We, the German Führer and Chancellor and the British Prime Minister, have had a further meeting today and are agreed in recognising that the question of Anglo-German relations is of the first importance for the two countries and for Europe.

We regard the agreement signed last night and the Anglo-German Naval Agreement as symbolic of the desire of our two peoples never to go to war with one another again.

We are resolved that the method of consultation shall be the method adopted to deal with any other questions that may concern our two countries, and we are determined to continue our efforts to remove possible sources of difference and thus to contribute to assure the peace of Europe.

September 30. 1938

The 'piece of paper' which Neville Chamberlain proudly displayed on his return to Britain after his meeting with Hitler

Neville Chamberlain at Heston Airport waving the 'piece of paper'

EXERCISES AND ACTIVITIES

SOURCE C

There was only a brief rest after the signing of the Agreement, for the next morning I was at Hitler's house to interpret the conversation with Chamberlain. Hitler looked quite different as he sat beside me, pale and moody. He listened absent-mindedly to Chamberlain's remarks about Anglo–German relations, disarmament and economic questions, contributing comparatively little to the conversation. Towards the end of the conversation Chamberlain drew the famous Anglo–German Declaration from his pocket ... Slowly, emphasising each word, I translated this statement to Hitler.

I did not share Chamberlain's impression, expressed in a private letter of his now published, that Hitler eagerly assented to this declaration. My own feeling was that he agreed to the wording with a certain reluctance, and I believe he appended his signature only to please Chamberlain, without promising himself any too much from the effects of the declaration.

Dr Paul Schmidt, *Hitler's Interpreter*,
edited by R. H. C. Steed, Heinemann, 1951

1 *Use the checklist on page 54 to test this document. In particular take careful note of the balance between facts and opinions in this account of a very important meeting.*

2 *You probably have as much evidence as any historian can have of what happened at this private meeting between Hitler and Chamberlain. Write an account of this meeting using the facts which are common to both sources and explain the different ways in which the two participants (Chamberlain and Schmidt) describe Hitler's attitude to the meeting.*

NEWSPAPERS AND MAGAZINES

Newspapers have been published in Britain for over 300 years. They were first taxed in 1712 and this made newspapers costly to buy. In 1797, the government raised the newspaper tax, called Stamp Duty, much higher in order to make it too expensive for ordinary people to buy a newspaper. They did not want newspapers putting revolutionary ideas about freedom, justice and fair play into the heads of the masses. When Stamp Duty was abolished in 1855 it paved the way for cheap newspapers. But it was not until the end of the century, however, that the first really cheap newspapers were published for the millions of people who could now read – thanks to the improvements in state education in the late nineteenth century.

The first of the popular newspapers, the *Daily Mail*, cost a halfpenny [about 0.2p] when it was first published in 1896. Since then many other popular cheap newspapers have been published as well, including the *Daily Express* (1900), *Daily Mirror* (1904) and the *Sun* (1969). The first illustrated weekly magazines were begun in the 1840s with the founding of *The Illustrated London News* and the humorous weekly *Punch*. Many of these magazines and newspapers relied on advertisements so that they could be sold cheaply.

Old newspapers and magazines are an invaluable source of historical evidence. Some, such as *The Times*, have been copied on to microfilm.

The great advantage of newspapers and magazines as historical sources is that they were written at the time as contemporary news reports. So they are primary historical sources. They were also written for ordinary people to read, so they are often more interesting and easier to read than official documents. This is not to say that they are always to be trusted. Far from it.

Many news reports were based on hearsay evidence, on biased reports from prejudiced journalists, or even taken straight from the columns of other newspapers. There is often no way of knowing what has been left out of a report or how reliable the anonymous writer was. Opinions are sometimes quoted as if they were facts. Many newspapers were (and still are) biased in favour of a particular political party. Popular newspapers often distort or colour the facts in order to make a news story more interesting to the paper's readers.

KING AND PEOPLE IN THE STREETS OF LONDON. ARMISTICE DAY, NOVEMBER 11, 1918

Front page of The Sphere, *16 November 1918. What does this magazine cover tell you about the way in which Londoners greeted the ending of the First World War?*

EXERCISES AND ACTIVITIES

Look at the cuttings opposite from three newspapers printed during the General Strike in May 1926.

1 *Go through each of these sources with the aid of the master checklist on page 54.*

2 *Which of these newspapers show political bias and in which direction? How do they try to convince their readers?*

3 *Compare the different ways in which all three newspapers appear to suggest that they know what the attitude of the general public was to the Strike.*

4 *Which newspaper would you have chosen to read had you wanted an unbiased account of the General Strike?*

A food convoy during the General Strike

SOURCE A

Daily Mail, Wednesday, 5 May 1926

Yesterday the general strike came into force, showing that there is no extremity of violence from which the persons behind this conspiracy will shrink. Their ostensible leaders, the Parliamentary politicians - whose business it is to act the role of decoy ducks and win the support of the muddle-headed and simple - may deal in sobstuff about the "terrible situation", and their reluctance to go to extremes. But while they talk, their followers act. While the House of Commons is treated to lacrimose speeches, the country is being "held up".

The British nation is eager to support its Government. It is waiting for its Government to act. It is looking to its Government to act. It is capable of any effort and of any sacrifice. But a nation cannot rally unless there is action; it cannot feel enthusiasm for a policy of sitting still. It never admired the policy of Kerensky, whose fault it was to imagine that words were the equivalent of deeds. When a fight is in progress (and the leaders of this strike have not hesitated to use the word "war") the only thing to do is to win it, not to think of what will happen if we do not win it. That is the policy which caused the failure of Jutland.

SOURCE B

The British Worker, Monday, 10 May 1926

NATION BEHIND THE T.U.C.

What a London Park Meeting Revealed

£55 COLLECTION

The quiet determination of the men on strike has impressed the outside public. The strikers' confidence and enthusiasm are contagious. They have spread to other sections of the nation.

"They don't look a bit like unemployed," remarked a young woman onlooker, who stood on the step of a West Norwood villa while a procession of transport strikers, be-medalled and in Sunday attire, marched in fours to Brockwell Park. The immense crowd in the park gave a clear indication of where the sympathies of the British nation lie in this dispute. Many of the crowd were trade unionists, including strikers and their families, but at least a third of them were of the class which the Press loves to call "the general public" - bank and insurance clerks, small shopkeepers, holders of season-tickets, dwellers in suburban villas.

THE END OF THE GENERAL STRIKE.

QUESTIONS OF PRAISE AND BLAME.

Everybody's first thought to-day must be one of profound satisfaction that the general strike is over. The British people have come with credit out of a severe ordeal. During an unprecedented struggle, extending over nine days, not a cartridge—not even a blank cartridge—has been fired by a soldier, and no single fatal collision has occurred between the strikers and the civil power. There has been no food shortage, no panic, and wonderfully little loss of temper on either side. In a fair trial of strength, which we hope may never be repeated, the nation has stood up to the general strike and overcome it.

Trade unionists, we believe, will agree that the calling of the general strike was a serious blunder. It placed their movement in a false position. Mr. Lloyd George, in a message sent out early yesterday before the settlement, stated the matter in two sentences. "If," he said,

"The trade unions inflict a defeat on the Government, it will be an encouragement to the extreme elements in Labour to resort in future to the general strike as a weapon of offence, whenever they find their purpose thwarted by the normal working of democratic institutions. Such a defeat would sooner or later end the experiment of popular government in these islands."

The time will come later to review the situation fully, and to decide the respective responsibilities of the Government and the T.U.C., but some things are clear already. The Government committed a disastrous blunder, when on the night of Sunday, May 2, after its basis for continuing to treat with its miners had been actually accepted by the T.U.C., it abruptly banged the door on negotiations. But for that, it seems certain that a settlement would have been reached without a strike. There was nothing unusual in it being deferred to the final 24 hours; settlements very often are. What was unusual, was that, by the Government's folly, the final 24 hours were suddenly made unavailable for negotiation. Mr. Baldwin has never been a cheap Prime Minister, but this was one of his costliest mistakes.

SOURCE C

The Daily Chronicle, Thursday, 13 May 1926

JOURNALS, DIARIES AND LETTERS

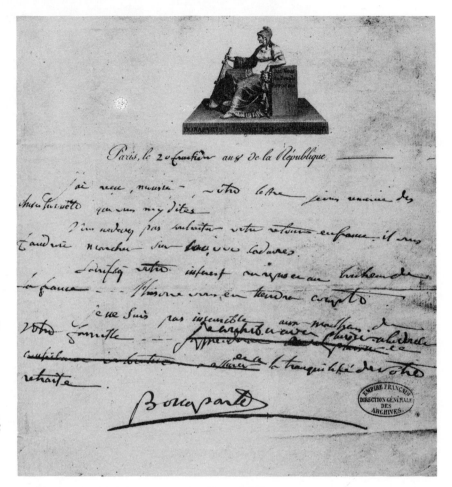

Can you pick out any of the French words in this letter written by Napoleon Bonaparte? The date may confuse you. It reads 'Paris, le 20 fructidor au 8 de la République'. The French Revolutionaries had introduced a new calendar. Fructidor was the month of fruit (from 19 August to 22 September). As you can see, the letter was written in the 8th year of the Republic – 1800. So 'le 20 fructidor au 8 de la République' was actually 7 September 1800.

Travel journals, diaries and letters are an important source of historical evidence. This is because they are primary sources. The descriptions are usually eyewitness accounts. The writers often recall conversations which were still fresh in the mind when they wrote them. The more interesting personal diaries and journals have been published; the most famous is probably the *Diary of Samuel Pepys* written in the 1660s.

The diary entries you will see will probably fall into two main groups. The first group contains the many diaries which have been published primarily because the diarist is or was someone famous (such as Gladstone or Dr Goebbels) or close to someone famous, such as an interpreter, husband or wife, or a private secretary.

The second group contains diaries which have been published because they throw unusual or fascinating light on the past through the eyes of ordinary people with no particular claim to fame. These diaries are almost always interesting and provide a valuable source of information about everyday life in the past. For instance, many diaries have been published which show what ordinary people thought and felt during the Second World War, such as Colin Perry's wartime diary *Boy in the Blitz* describing the German air raids on London in 1940 (see page 38) and the similar diary by Mathilde Wolff-Monckeberg, *On the Other Side*, which describes the Allied air raids on Hamburg (see page 45).

Collections of letters written by famous people, such as the private letters of Neville Chamberlain to his two sisters (see page 55) have also been published. These are particularly useful where the letters are addressed to other important people and their replies have been published as well, such as those between the American President Franklin Roosevelt and other statesmen, such as Winston Churchill. Letters between statesmen and politicians often help historians to discover the reasons why actions were taken in the past. It helps us to understand their motives.

At first glance, journals, diaries and letters seem to be an ideal historical source. Those by famous people are often especially interesting where they tell us why certain actions were taken, and what the writer thought as well as what he or she did. But there are a number of drawbacks. Famous people know that their letters and diaries will probably be published for everyone to read. This is why they are often written as if the writer is attempting to justify or excuse certain actions. It is difficult to be certain that the writer is being honest. The diaries of ordinary people are often more revealing. Samuel Pepys tells far more in his diary than he told people to their faces. It is also a fact that the participants at a meeting can often come away with very different impressions (as you saw when Chamberlain met Hitler in 1938 – see pages 55–58). The extract which follows is taken from a diary by an American journalist who was in charge of the foreign service of *The New York Times*. In his job he met most of the world's leading politicians and statesmen of the 1930s, 1940s and 1950s.

> . . . in contemplating my own diary, I remember how inaccurate diaries can be. Once I played cards with Eisenhower, Harriman, Gruenther and Dan Kimball, United States Secretary of the Navy, while all discussed the memoirs of James Forrestal, first Secretary of Defence. They had attended a meeting referred to in the book and each agreed that Forrestal's account was wrong. But when I asked what, then, was the true version, all promptly disagreed among themselves.
>
> C. L. Sulzberger, *A Long Row of Candles: Memoirs and Diaries 1934–1954*, Macdonald, 1969

EXERCISES AND ACTIVITIES

Go through the master checklist on page 54 for each of these three sources in turn.

Mr Gladstone addressing the crowd from the balcony of Lord Rosebery's house in George Street, Edinburgh. The Graphic, April 1880.

SOURCE A

March 31. 1880

Gentlemen,

It has not been in my power to visit you individually; but you will agree with me that this contest is essentially patriotic, and is lifted far above the level of any question of personal attentions.

At home, in uphold diligent and careful legislation against neglect; economy and prudence against financial disorder; careful regard for the

Constitution against invasion of the rights of Parliament: and abroad, not, as is absurdly alleged, a rule of inaction, but sympathy with freedom, and strict observance of justice and of honour, as the most vital of all British interests.

Before you read these lines, my name may have headed the poll in the great town of Leeds. But, however great the honour, it is unsought by me. My position will remain unaltered, and my regard and desire solely directed to the suffrages of Midlothian.

Part of a letter from Mr Gladstone to the electors of Midlothian dated 31 March 1880

SOURCE B   ENTRY FROM MR GLADSTONE'S DIARY, 5 APRIL 1880

> Drove into Edinburgh about four. At 7.20 Mr Reid brought the figures of the poll – Gladstone 1579; Dalkeith 1368; quite satisfactory. Soon after 15 000 people being gathered in George Street, I spoke very shortly from the windows, and Rosebery followed, excellently well. Home about 10.

1 *Copy out Gladstone's letter. Can you read every word? What did Gladstone think was the most important thing about the 1880 General Election?*

2 *What criticisms did he make of the Conservative government led by Lord Beaconsfield (formerly Benjamin Disraeli)? How did a Liberal Government led by Gladstone propose to deal with these issues?*

3 *Why did he begin his election address with the single word 'Gentlemen'?*

4 *Only 1579 people voted for him (out of a total poll of 2947 voters). Yet 15 000 people crowded into George Street to hear him speak. What does this tell you about the electoral system in 1880?*

The third source (below) is taken from a diary which was written between 1899 and 1900 but was not discovered until seventy years later. It was written by Solomon Tshekisho Plaatje. He was a black South African who later went on to become an important writer and political leader. In 1912 he became the first secretary of the South African National Congress, the forerunner of the African National Congress. He was a member of the Barolong people, had been educated at Mission schools, and could write in Dutch and English as well as in South African languages, such as Xhosa, Tswana and Zulu. His diary is of great historical interest because he was living in Mafeking at the time of the famous siege during the Boer War.

SOURCE C   Wednesday 24th January 1900

> There is a proclamation by the Colonel R. S. S. Baden-Powell that no food stores of any kind would in the future be sold to the public; and white people are now going to buy food in rations and be compelled to buy small quantities, the same as blacks. I have often heard the black folk say money is useless as you cannot eat it when you feel hungry, and now I have lived it and experienced it. The thing appears to be going from bad to worse. The big gun is still hammering away at us. It was particularly cruel today. One of its shells hit on the Market Square this morning. It bumped right up in the air and singled out old Moshuchwe's hut (one-and-a-half miles away): after its decline it entered the hut from the back, decapitating two women and wounding three brothers severely and one not dangerously. The old boy was not there.

> *The Boer War Diary of Sol T. Plaatje,*
> edited by John L. Comaroff, Macmillan, 1973

NB The full ration of food was 2s [10p] for a European man; 1s [5p] for a European woman; and 6d [2.5p] for a European child under 14 years. The full ration of food for a Black African man was 6d [2.5p].

5   *How did the siege of Mafeking directly affect the people who lived there?*

6   *How does this diary entry show that Black Africans were regarded as second class citizens?*

7   *How many people lived in Moshuchwe's hut?*

8   *How did 'the Colonel' become known the world over some years after the seige at Mafeking?*

MEMOIRS AND ORAL EVIDENCE

The recollections of old people about their early lives are a form of historical evidence. When your grandparents tell stories about their life in the Second World War, you are listening to history. Oral evidence is memories of the past which are told to the historian rather than written down as memoirs. It often gives an immediate and vivid insight into the lives and attitudes of ordinary people, such as a coal miner talking about the General Strike, or a suffragette describing her life in prison. It is usually recorded first on cassette, tape, or video but may be written down at a later date. Oral evidence is increasingly recognised for its important contribution to our understanding of the past.

Memoirs, on the other hand, are usually written by better known people, such as a former prime minister or an admiral. The main difference compared with oral history is that they are written down instead of being spoken. They are almost always backed up in detail by documentary evidence, such as diaries, letters and official documents.

Both types of recollection – the spoken history and the written memoir – may be inaccurate and unreliable historical sources. This is because they depend heavily on human memory, which may or may not be faulty. Older people often tend to remember the past as being either much better or much worse than the present. Only rarely do they seem to think of it as being the same! If people were poor, they were much poorer than today. If they were happy, they were much happier than today! Not surprisingly, people recalling past events tend to justify their own actions. Writers of memoirs may skip over their mistakes and omit the less successful or more shameful periods of their lives. Above all, beware of the razor-sharp recollection of events which happened fifty or sixty years ago. This is not eyewitness evidence you can always trust.

EXERCISES AND ACTIVITIES

The following passage is an extract from an interview with a Scottish general practitioner who worked in West Lothian in the 1920s and early 1930s. He describes how the introduction of new drugs after 1938, such drugs as sulphonamides and, later, penicillin, transformed medical practice. Now diseases which would have brought almost certain death could be cured easily.

I started in general practice in West Lothian. In the country districts we had three small hamlets to look after – collections of miners' dwellings. At least two of these villages – only seventeen miles from Edinburgh – still had dry closets. When I went on my rounds on a morning I would see the night soil man going round with his horse and cart. They had no electric lighting in these cottages; it was all candles and oil lamps. One delivered mothers and attended children in these conditions.

I'm not criticising the family doctors – after all, I was one in the 1920s. But the opening of infant welfare clinics meant that the mother could get medical advice without payment. Otherwise she would have to go to the private doctor and pay. We attended several working class people in Scotland. They were very nice folk indeed and they scraped and saved so that they could always pay the doctor when he called.

The impact of the new drugs began just before the Second World War. In the City Fever Hospital in Newcastle in 1938 I treated my first patient with some stuff called 'Prontosil'. It was the forerunner of all the sulphonamides. The result was quite dramatic. These drugs revolutionised the treatment of mothers and children. And now we have a whole range of drugs.

When I was working with my brother in Scotland we had a whooping cough outbreak. We knew that no matter what we prescribed and no matter what we did we were likely to lose at least one child. There was no specific remedy as we have it today with modern penicillins.

1 *What does this extract tell you about living conditions and health care in mining areas of West Lothian in the 1920s and 1930s?*

2 *How had health care improved by the Second World War?*

3 *Use the checklist on page 54 (Master Checklist – Documentary Evidence) to test this extract.*

Use a cassette recorder to collect oral evidence which you can use when you are studying a topic in recent history, such as the General Strike in 1926, schools in the 1930s, bombing raids in World War Two, or the Cuban missile crisis of 1962. Choose a theme which your older relatives can talk about. When you have made the tape recording, use the master checklist on page 24 to test the reliability of your historical sources.

USING PROPAGANDA AND ADVERTS

Propaganda is anything which deliberately sets out to persuade you to accept only one particular viewpoint, attitude, or set of facts, irrespective of the truth. At its worst it is a campaign by ruthless people, such as the Nazis, to distort the truth in order to win backing for a war or a campaign of persecution. At its best, it is an effective advertisement designed to persuade people to give up a habit, such as cigarette smoking, which experts believe could damage their health. Nowadays television is the most powerful medium through which to advertise or disseminate propaganda. The Nazi minister for propaganda, Dr Josef Goebbels, recognised the power of broadcasting in the 1930s, long before it was effectively used in Britain or America.

German poster of the 1930s – 'ONE PEOPLE – ONE COUNTRY – ONE LEADER'

'All Germany hears the Führer with the People's Radio'

Propaganda is a valuable source of historical evidence, since it often tells us a lot about the way in which the great dictators of the twentieth century held on to power and how they managed to get popular support for their policies. Posters, advertisements, broadcasts, films, official publications, and speeches helped to surround the leader – Führer, Duce, or Caudillo – with an almost religious atmosphere of mystery, awe, and power. Mussolini revered the days of the ancient Roman Empire when Italy dominated Europe, North Africa and the Middle East. This is why the Fascists deliberately chose the ancient Roman symbol of authority – the *fasces* (a bundle of rods grouped around an axe) as their symbol of power. Mussolini liked to speak to a crowd standing in front of a classical building or statue. The Fascist salute – the upraised arm – was used by soldiers in Ancient Rome. You can see this theme repeated time and again in Fascist propaganda, such as a poster showing the Italian army marching into Abyssinia with Roman legions supporting them in the background.

What does this photograph tell you about Mussolini and the Italian Fascists?

The Nazis used simple propaganda slogans to portray Hitler as a Messiah who had come to save Germany. In 1937 Dr Ley, a leading Nazi politician, was quoted as telling an audience:

> Everything comes from Adolf Hitler. His faith is our faith, and therefore our daily prayer is: I believe in Adolf Hitler alone!

Rudolf Hess (Hitler's deputy) in his Christmas speech on 24 December 1940 went even further:

> On this Christmas, our prayer is: 'Lord Almighty, Thou hast given us the Führer: Thou hast blessed his struggle by a mighty victory...'

EXERCISES AND ACTIVITIES

1 *What was the propaganda message conveyed to the Russian people by this sculpture entitled 'The struggle for peace'? How does it depict Stalin?*

British advertisement in December 1914 aimed at people wealthy enough to employ servants

5 Questions to those who employ male servants

1. HAVE you a Butler, Groom, Chauffeur, Gardener, or Gamekeeper serving you who, at this moment should be serving your King and Country?

2. Have you a man serving at your table who should be serving a gun?

3. Have you a man digging your garden who should be digging trenches?

4. Have you a man driving your car who should be driving a transport wagon?

5. Have you a man preserving your game who should be helping to preserve your Country?

A great responsibility rests on you. Will you sacrifice your personal convenience for your Country's need?

Ask your men to enlist **TO-DAY.**

The address of the nearest Recruiting Office can be obtained at any Post Office.

God Save the King.

2 *What does this advertisement tell you about Britain in 1914? Who was being asked to make a sacrifice?*

3   *How does this famous 'Wanted' poster make its point? Why do you think it was published? Does it tell us anything about the causes of the Second World War?*

WANTED!

FOR MURDER . . . FOR KIDNAPPING . . . FOR THEFT AND FOR ARSON

Can be recognised full face by habitual scowl. Rarely smiles Talks rapidly, and when angered screams like a child.

ADOLF HITLER
ALIAS
Adolf Schicklegruber, Adolf Hittler or Hidler

Last heard of in Berlin, September 3, 1939. Aged fifty, height 5ft. 8½in., dark hair, frequently brushes one lock over left forehead. Blue eyes. Sallow complexion, stout build, weighs about 11st. 3lb. Suffering from acute monomania, with periodic fits of melancholia. Frequently bursts into tears when crossed. Harsh, guttural voice, and has a habit of raising right hand to shoulder level. DANGEROUS!

Profile from a recent photograph. Black moustache. Jowl inclines to fatness. Wide nostrils. Deep-set, menacing eyes.

FOR MURDER Wanted for the murder of over a thousand of his fellow countrymen on the night of the Blood Bath, June 30, 1934. Wanted for the murder of countless political opponents in concentration camps.

He is indicted for the murder of Jews, Germans, Austrians, Czechs, Spaniards and Poles. He is now urgently wanted for homicide against citizens of the British Empire.

Hitler is a gunman who shoots to kill. He acts first and talks afterwards.

No appeals to sentiment can move him. This gangster, surrounded by armed hoodlums, is a natural killer. The reward for his apprehension, dead or alive, is the peace of mankind.

FOR KIDNAPPING Wanted for the kidnapping of Dr. Kurt Schuschnigg, late Chancellor of Austria. Wanted for the kidnapping of Pastor Niemoller, a heroic martyr who was not afraid to put God before Hitler. Wanted for the attempted kidnapping of Dr. Benes, late President of Czechoslovakia. The kidnapping tendencies of this established criminal are marked and violent. The symptoms before an attempt are threats, blackmail and ultimatums. He offers his victims the alternatives of complete surrender or timeless incarceration in the horrors of concentration camps.

FOR THEFT Wanted for the larceny of eighty millions of Czech gold in March, 1939. Wanted for the armed robbery of material resources of the Czech State. Wanted for the stealing of Memelland. Wanted for robbing mankind of peace, of humanity, and for the attempted assault on civilisation itself. This dangerous lunatic masks his raids by spurious appeals to honour, to patriotism and to duty. At the moment when his protestations of peace and friendship are at their most vehement, he is most likely to commit his smash and grab.

His tactics are known and easily recognised. But Europe has already been wrecked and plundered by the depredations of this armed thug who smashes in without scruple.

FOR ARSON Wanted as the incendiary who started the Reichstag fire on the night of February 27, 1933. This crime was the key point, and the starting signal for a series of outrages and brutalities that are unsurpassed in the records of criminal degenerates. As a direct and immediate result of this calculated act of arson, an innocent dupe, Van der Lubbe, was murdered in cold blood. But as an indirect outcome of this carefully-planned offence, Europe itself is ablaze. The fires that this man has kindled cannot be extinguished until he himself is apprehended—dead or alive!

THIS RECKLESS CRIMINAL IS WANTED—DEAD OR ALIVE!

Propaganda page in the Daily Mirror published in London on the day after the outbreak of war in September 1939

EVIDENCE FROM FICTION

Fiction simply means anything which has been invented or made up. Fiction can take many different forms. It includes stories, plays, novels, poems, ballads, rhymes, and the words to songs.

Fiction is often rooted in fact. Authors often base their writings on things they have seen themselves in real life. There is little point in trying to get readers involved in the plot of a story if the descriptions of politicians, ordinary people, houses, shops, working conditions, and clothes of the characters do not ring true as well. The stories are fictional, but the way of life described is usually typical of its time. This can be confirmed by comparing written accounts in novels and stories with factual descriptions, photographs, and pictures.

Fiction also throws light on the way in which people behaved, such as their manners and their customs. It can help us to understand how people spoke and their attitudes to servants or to employers. Descriptions of political events, such as strikes and election meetings, are often particularly vivid because they are written by excellent writers who knew how to make a scene come to life. This is why fiction, including foreign fiction in translation, can be a useful source of historical evidence.

Like most historical sources, however, there are drawbacks. If a writer, such as Charles Dickens, felt strongly about an injustice he often exaggerated the problem, or based his story on a particularly bad case (such as the schoolmaster Wackford Squeers in *Nicholas Nickleby*). There is a danger that the writer of fiction may make a particular situation appear to be much worse, or much better, than it really was in fact.

Going through the Checklist

You can apply the same checks to fiction as you would to a factual historical source. Read the following extracts from A. J. Cronin's novel, *Adventures in Two Worlds*. Cronin was born in Dumbartonshire in 1896. After World War One he studied Medicine at Glasgow University, and practised as a doctor before becoming a novelist. *Adventures in Two Worlds* was published in 1952 and is about a medical student who failed to achieve his ambition to become a surgeon. Much of the book is based on the author's own experiences.

In this first extract, the young doctor has just joined the practice of old, experienced Dr Cameron in the Scottish village of Tannochbrae. Dr Cameron is complaining about being called out to a patient.

'I can't be hard on a poor devil like that. It's a weakness I never seem to get over. He owes me for his wife's last confinement – he'll never pay it. But I'll get out the gig, drive seven miles, see the child, drive seven miles back. And what do you think I'll mark against him in the book? One and six – if I don't forget. And what does it matter if I do forget? He'll never pay me a red bawbee in any case. Oh, dammit to hell! What a life for a man who loves fiddles!'

Silence again; then I ventured:

'Shall I do the call?'

Arriving at the remote cottage, the doctor finds that his first case is a child with diphtheria.

I felt myself so young, so utterly inept and inexperienced in the face of the great elemental forces which surged within the room. I said in a manner wholly unimpressive:

'The boy has diphtheria. The membrane is blocking the larynx. There's only one thing to do. Operate. Open the windpipe below the obstruction.' . . .

I swabbed the skin of the child's throat with iodine. I took a clean towel and laid it across those glazing eyes. The case was far beyond an anaesthetic; madness to think of using it. Jamie was holding the oil lamp near. Setting my teeth, I picked up the lancet. I made the incision with a steady hand, but I felt my legs trembling beneath me. A deep incision, but not deep enough. I must go deeper, deeper. . . . The child would die; they would say that I had killed him, I cursed myself in spirit. Beads of sweat broke out on my brow, as I remembered, suddenly, MacEwan's fatal words: 'You will never be a surgeon.' . . .

For one sickening instant I had a quick vision of all the operations I had known – of the cold, immaculate precision of the Infirmary theatre, and then, by frightful contrast, this struggling, desperate thing dying under my knife on a kitchen table, by the flare of an oil lamp, while the wind howled and stormed outside. Oh, God, I prayed, help me, help me now. . . .

And then under my searching knife the thin white tube sprang into view. Swiftly I incised it, and in the instant the child's gasping ceased. Instead, a long clear breath of air went in through the opening.

A.J. Cronin, *Adventures In Two Worlds*, NEL edition, 1977, pp 42–46

1   *What does the source tell you about the past?*

It describes medical practice in rural Scotland in the period between the two world wars.

2   *What is the origin of the source? What type of evidence is it? Is it likely to be reliable?*

It is from a novel by A.J. Cronin who had himself worked as a doctor in Scotland in the period about which he is writing.

3   *Why was the source written?*

As a novel.

4   *When was the source written? Is it a primary source dating from the time of the event it describes? Or is it a secondary source?*

It was written in 1952, about twenty years after the period described. It could be primary evidence, if the author had experienced a similar case and had kept a record of it, but we cannot tell this from the extract.

Checkpoints 5, 6, 7, 8 and 10 do not apply since the story was written as fiction and is not meant to be read as a factual account of events.

9   *Are there any obvious mistakes or errors of fact in the extract? Which statements are supported by facts you know about from other sources? Does anything in the extract contradict other sources or facts which you know to be true?*

Much of this extract is supported by the evidence of the Scottish doctor on page 67 (Memoirs and Oral Evidence). Both refer to the poverty of their patients and the hardship caused by the need to pay doctors' bills. Both show how children then suffered from deadly illnesses which could later be cured or prevented by drugs; and how doctors had to treat their patients in primitive conditions in cottages lit by oil lamps.

EXERCISES AND ACTIVITIES

The following extract is from *The Expedition of Humphry Clinker*, a novel by Tobias Smollett, published in 1771. It describes the High Street in Edinburgh's Old Town.

> Considering its fine pavement, its width, and the lofty houses on each side, this would be undoubtedly one of the noblest streets in Europe, if an ugly mass of mean buildings, called the Lucken-Booths, had not thrust itself, by what accident I know not, into the

middle of the way, like Middle-Row in Holborn. The city stands upon two hills, and the bottom between them; and, with all its defects, may very well pass for the capital of a moderate kingdom. It is full of people, and continually resounds with the noise of coaches and other carriages, for luxury as well as commerce. As far as I can perceive, here is no want of provisions. . . .

The water is brought in leaden pipes from a mountain in the neighbourhood, to a cistern on the Castle-hill, from whence it is distributed to public conduits in different parts of the city. From these it is carried in barrels on the backs of male and female porters, up two, three, four, five, six, seven, and eight pairs of stairs, for the use of particular families. Every storey is a complete house, occupied by a separate family; and the stair being common to them all, is generally left in a very filthy condition; a man must tread with great circumspection to get safe housed with unpolluted shoes. . . .

You are no stranger to their method of discharging all their impurities from their windows at a certain hour of the night, as the custom is in Spain, Portugal and some parts of France and Italy – a practice to which I can by no means be reconciled.

Tobias Smollett, *Humphry Clinker*, Penguin edition, 1988, p. 254

1   *What can you learn from this extract about the houses in Edinburgh's Old Town in the late eighteenth century?*

2   *What would be the advantages and disadvantages of living in Edinburgh?*

3   *You might like to compare this extract from a novel with other eighteenth century sources about Edinburgh – for example, Daniel Defoe's* A Tour Through The Whole Island of Great Britain; *Edward Topham's letters; or Hugo Arnot's* History of Edinburgh. *How reliable does Smollett's description appear to be as a historical source?*

4   *Now go through the master checklist on page 54 (Master Checklist – Documentary Evidence).*

EVIDENCE ON MAPS

Maps and plans are another useful source of historical evidence. The first really accurate maps of Britain were published by the Ordnance Survey in the early 1800s. Maps of a town or district from different periods of time are easy to compare, especially if they have been drawn to scale. Maps like these are primary sources. By comparing maps at different periods of time you can find out when a town began to grow outwards. You can compare the information you gain from old maps with information from census returns showing when and how the town's population grew.

Checklist — Maps and Plans

When you first use an old map or plan there are certain checks you should make first before using it as a historical source.

1   *When was the map drawn? What does it show? If it is a special map why was it drawn?*

2   *Is the map accurately drawn? Has it got a scale? If not, work out the scale for yourself. Compare measurements on the old map between three landmarks (e.g. churches) and then compare them with the same measurements on a modern map. In this way you can tell if the map was drawn roughly to scale or not (since the three landmarks will not have moved their position since the date when the old map was drawn).*

3   *What is the particular value of the map (if any) as a source of historical information?*

Going through the Checklist

The maps on the next two pages are taken from *The Pupil's Empire Atlas*, a text book for British schools, published in 1925.

1   *Why were the maps drawn? What do they show? If they are special maps, why were they drawn?*

The maps were drawn in 1925 for the use of British children studying in schools. They show Scotland's manufactures, imports and exports, and holiday resorts at that time.

2 *Are the maps accurately drawn? Do they have a scale? If not, work out the scale for yourself.*

The maps are accurate enough for their purpose. They have a scale of 1.8 cm : 60 miles.

3 *What is the particular value of the maps (if any) as a source of historical information.*

These maps would be a very useful source of information if you were studying the Scottish economy in the 1920s.

Map A shows that Scotland's main industries were still the 'old staples' of the Industrial Revolution – coal, iron and steel, textiles and shipbuilding. Map B indicates Scotland's imports and exports: she imported mainly raw materials and exported mainly manufactured goods. Map C shows Scotland's chief holiday resorts in 1925.

Useful comparisons might be made with the Scottish economy now. The old staples have continued to decline since the 1920s and there is much greater dependence on service industries. Scotland is still popular with tourists from Britain and other countries and although the tourist industry has grown since the twenties, the same areas are still popular. Many more Scots now take holidays abroad.

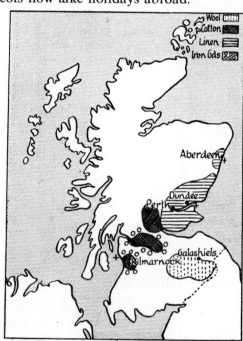

MANUFACTURES. The coal of the Scotch coalfield supplies many factories. Glasgow, like Lancashire, is wet. and so is suitable for the cotton industry. Iron and steel works are numerous, and the mouth of the Clyde is lined with shipyards which make the largest ships. The lower portion of the Clyde Valley is a hive of industry. Of less importance are the linen manufactures around Dundee and the cloth factories of the Tweed. The map above will show why cloth has long been made on the Tweed.

B

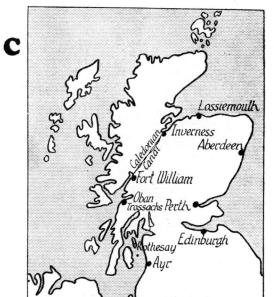

C

IMPORTS AND EXPORTS. The important business with England is not shown on this map, but, like England, Scotland needs food and raw material—cotton, flax and timber—for its manufactures, some of which are subsequently exported to various parts of the world. The famous shipbuilding yards of the Clyde export ships of all types and sizes to every part of the world.

HOLIDAY RESORTS. Because of its magnificent scenery, Scotland is visited by thousands of tourists annually from other countries. Edinburgh (a most beautiful city), The Trossachs (popularised by Sir W. Scott), The Western Lochs and Islands, are the most popular. Many Scotch people go to the East Coast towns and particularly to Rothesay on the Island of Bute on the West Coast. Ayr—Robert Burns.

EXERCISES AND ACTIVITIES

Study the maps of India on page 80. They are also taken from *The Pupil's Empire Atlas*, 1925.

1   Assess the maps using the checklist.

2   List India's chief imports and exports.

3   How important was India for the British economy in 1925?

4   What attitudes towards India and the Empire might a British pupil learn from these maps?

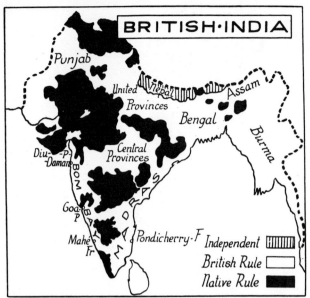

BRITISH INDIA. Britain has fought many battles to gain and retain India which is the home of not one, but many peoples, and their constant struggles with one another made trade impossible. Little by little Britain was compelled to assume control, until now practically the whole of India is under our sway. The blank portion shows the parts directly ruled by this country. Some provinces (shown black) have their own native prince with a certain amount of independence under British guidance. In the North is Kashmir, Rajputana below that, Hyderabad in the Deccan, Mysore below, Travancore in the extreme South.

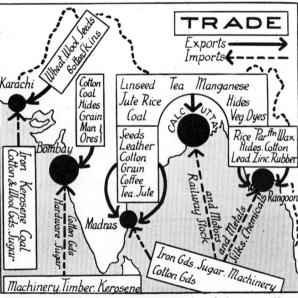

TRADE. India imports over £200,000,000 of goods in a year, 60 per cent. of which comes from the United Kingdom, with about 5 per cent. each from Japan, U.S.A., Java and Germany. Exports exceed the above amount. 22 per cent. go to the U.K., 13 per cent. to Japan with U.S.A. and Germany next on the list. Calcutta, the chief port (on the Hoogly, one of the mouths of the Ganges), has a yearly tonnage of nearly 7 million tons. The size of the circles indicates approximately the tonnage which enters and leaves the ports. Note particularly the growing importance of Rangoon.

FACTS FROM PICTURES

'The Seven Cranes', by the British war artist Muirhead Bone, shows the revival of the ship-building industry under the stimulus of the First World War.

Pictures created shortly after an event are called *contemporary pictures*. Historians often use them as primary sources. They include paintings, sketches, cartoons, drawings, engravings, pictures on pottery, pictures on stamps, pictures on song sheets, statues, carvings, etc.

The main drawback to the use of contemporary pictures is that we cannot always be certain that the picture created by the artist actually portrays real things. The concern of many artists in the past was to produce a pleasing picture which was well composed and well drawn or painted. The artist who drew a battle scene often did so from the point of view of one of the participating armies. Since artists have the freedom to emphasize the good or bad points in a scene, two illustrators depicting the same scene or event can sometimes produce two very different pictures.

We cannot always be certain that the pictures we see were actually drawn or painted on the spot or even that they were based on sketches actually made in the field. Some illustrations have been drawn from photographs, or based on newspaper reports and eyewitness accounts. Many detailed and lifelike pictures have been 'imagined' by the artist in a studio. As a consequence we cannot always be sure that realistic pictures of people, places, and events are the eyewitness primary sources they may at first appear to suggest.

A further drawback is that in many cases you will not be able to find out much about the origins of the contemporary pictures you see. This is partly because many pictures have been drawn by anonymous or unknown artists and partly because pictures are often reproduced in books without giving an indication of their actual origin.

Political cartoons based on recent events are another important source of information used by historians. They often sum up a controversy, crisis, or great event in a sketch and a short caption, such as the *Punch* cartoon 'Whose Turn Next?' on the next page, which depicts Dame Europa warning her pupils (Czechoslovakia, Hungary, Romania, and Poland) that 'The Göblins will get you if you don't watch out!' As you can see, Austria had already been taken by then (May 1938). This was after the Anschluss (when the Nazis seized power in Austria) but well before the Sudetenland was handed over to Hitler later in the same year (see pages 136–8).

Punch, *18 May 1938*

WHOSE TURN NEXT?

Checklist — **Pictures from the Past**

You will not always be able to answer every checkpoint in this list when you study a picture. This is because most pictures are printed without giving full details of when, where, why, and how they were produced, and by whom.

You can see how each of these checkpoints applies to the pictures on pages 85–89.

1   *Does the picture attempt realistically to portray people, events, buildings, etc., or does it poke fun at them by means of a cartoon or an exaggerated drawing (called a caricature)?*

2   *What does the picture show? What does it tell us about the past?*

3   *When was the picture drawn? Was it drawn at roughly the same time as the event or feature it depicts? Is it a primary source? If no date is given, can you estimate roughly the date when it was drawn from the clothes worn by the people in the picture, from styles of vehicle (such as motor cars), or from other clues?*

4   *Why was the picture drawn or painted? Was it simply an illustration (e.g. to accompany a news item or to illustrate a book) or is there any reason to think the artist was using the picture to make you feel in a certain way about the events or people depicted? For instance, was it drawn or painted to make you want to protest against an injustice, or to feel excited, or sad, or nostalgic for an old way of life, or patriotic, or self-satisfied, or envious of someone else's way of life?*

5   *Does the picture show something which could not be shown in any other way, such as the interior of a courtroom where photographs are not permitted?*

6   *Even if it looks like a realistic picture is there any reason to think it is a product of the artist's imagination rather than a portrayal of an actual scene or event?*

7   *If the picture is a cartoon, what was the artist getting at? What does the cartoon tell you about the topic, events or people portrayed? What does it tell you about the attitude of the artist who drew the cartoon or of the magazine which published it?*

1942 cartoon by David Low of Gandhi in prison. Gandhi was imprisoned in 1942 for supporting the Indian Congress Party's campaign to force the British to 'Quit India'. Gandhi always urged his followers to use non-violent methods. In prison he spun and made cloth; this emphasised his belief that Indians could become economically self-sufficient and his faith in traditional values. Low had met Gandhi eleven years earlier.

What does 'a shroud for liberty' mean? In what ways does the cartoon convey Gandhi's political beliefs?

Below *Advertisement for 'Uncle Tom's Cabin' and a picture of Topsy and Eva from the book.*

Harriet Beecher Stowe's novel 'Uncle Tom's Cabin' had a great impact on American public opinion, turning many against the system of slavery used on southern plantations.

What does the advertisement at the bottom of page 85 tell you about the book's popularity? What message does the picture of Eva and Topsy convey?

Freedmen's bureau, Memphis

After emancipation, many former slaves had no work or houses. Here they queue to have their cases heard. Many were bitter that the northern politicians' promises of 'forty acres and a mule' for every Negro were not kept. What impression of the freedmen does the artist give here?

*Sir Harry Lauder by Henry Mayo Bateman,
1915*

*Harry Lauder was a music hall comedian of
the early twentieth century. What
impressions did he give of the Scots to the
English audiences?*

Local Defence Volunteer (Home Guard, 1940)

*The Local Defence Volunteers (later called the
Home Guard) were set up during World War Two.
They were volunteers who could not serve in the
regular armed forces and were expected to defend
their localities in the event of a German invasion.*

*Can you tell that this man is not a regular soldier?
How old do you think he is?*

YESTERDAY - THE TRENCHES   TO-DAY-UNEMPLOYED

Above *Labour Party election poster after World War One*
Below *Conservative Party election poster, 1979*

To whom does the Labour poster try to appeal? Who is blamed for unemployment in the Conservative poster? How effective do you think the posters would be in winning votes?

THE RETREAT OF THE RED PACK

This Punch *cartoon which was published on 22 October 1919 celebrates a Red Army defeat and depicts the Bolshevik wolves running for cover. What does this cartoon tell you about British attitudes to the Bolshevik Revolution?*

Going through the Checklist

SOURCE A

THE OLD MAN OF THE STEPPES.
'We've reached the fifth milestone, little brother,
but the burden isn't any easier yet.'

Cartoon from Punch *published on 11 January 1933*

Look at Source A at the bottom of the previous page.

1 *Does the picture attempt to portray realistically people, events, buildings, etc., or does it poke fun at them by means of a cartoon or an exaggerated drawing (called a caricature)?*

It is a cartoon which makes fun of the Communist Revolution in the Soviet Union.

2 *What does the picture show? What does it tell us about the past?*

It depicts Josef Stalin, the Russian dictator, riding on the back of a Soviet peasant. Stalin is carrying a hammer and a sickle (the well-known symbol of the USSR) together with a whip. They have just reached the 'fifth milestone' marked with the Roman numeral V on the milestone at the side of a very rough and stony path. Stalin tells the peasant that they have reached the target – the fifth milestone – 'but the burden isn't any easier yet'. This is a reference to Stalin's Five Year Plans which set production targets for industry and for the people. The cartoon shows the attitude of many people in Britain to the Soviet Union at that time.

3 *When was the picture drawn? Was it drawn at roughly the same time as the event or feature it depicts? Is it a primary source?*

It was drawn for the issue of *Punch* dated 11 January 1933. The First Five Year Plan was started in October 1928 and the Second Five Year Plan in November 1933. So it is a primary source.

4 *Why was the picture drawn or painted?*

To make the point that Stalin was not relaxing his grip on the Soviet Union. Life was not to be any easier for the Russians in the next five years either.

Checkpoints 5 and 6 do not apply.

7 *If the picture is a cartoon, what was the artist getting at? What does the cartoon tell you about the events or the people portrayed? What does it tell you about the attitude of the artist who drew the cartoon or of the magazine which published it?*

[See response to checkpoint 2.]

SOURCE B

Punch *cartoon,*
15 April 1848

"NOT SO VERY UNREASONABLE!!! EH?"

1   *Does the picture attempt realistically to portray people, events, buildings, etc., or does it poke fun at them by means of a cartoon or an exaggerated drawing (called a caricature)?*

It is a cartoon from *Punch*.

2   *What does the picture show? What does it tell us about the past?*

It shows a working man (a Chartist) delivering the Charter to the prime minister in 1848. The Charter was a massive petition containing millions of signatures, most of them from the working class. They were demanding voting rights, e.g. one man, one vote.

3   *When was the picture drawn? Was it drawn at roughly the same time as the event or feature it depicts? Is it a primary source?*

This is a primary source since it was published on 15 April 1848.

4   *Why was the picture drawn or painted?*

It was drawn at the time of a great Chartist meeting in London which the government feared might lead to a serious riot, if not a rebellion. To counter any such danger they put the Duke of Wellington in charge of the police and army in the city.

Checkpoints 5 and 6 do not apply.

7   *If the picture is a cartoon, what was the artist getting at? What does the cartoon tell you about the events or the people portrayed? What does it tell you about the attitude of the artist who drew the cartoon or of the magazine which published it?*

The artist says that the demands of the Chartists were not so very unreasonable and that the fears of the Government were unfounded.

EXERCISES AND ACTIVITIES

The Dinner Hour,
Wigan

This picture was painted in 1874 by the painter Eyre Crowe. It was probably posed and painted in his studio. The artist may well have used sketches made in the streets of Wigan before working on the painting. It may or may not depict actual mills and factories.

1   *Go through the checklist on page 84. What value would you put on this painting as a source of historical information?*

'*Lost in London*', The Illustrated London News, *7 January 1888*

Punch cartoon,
22 September 1888

BLIND-MAN'S BUFF

Two entirely different attitudes to the London Metropolitan Police are depicted in these two drawings, both dating from the same year, 1888. The cartoon, 'Blind-man's buff' reflected the impatience and fear of members of the public at Scotland Yard's inability to find the Jack the Ripper murderer.

2 *Go through the checklist on page 84 with each of the pictures. What value would you put on each one as a source of historical information? What does it tell you about the attitudes of people in Victorian London to the police?*

FACTS FROM PHOTOGRAPHS

Skye crofters planting potatoes, 1880s

Photographs like this have given the historian a new and often very accurate source of evidence. When we look at it we can feel like eye-witnesses. It is true that we do not see the picture in colour. Nor do we see the movement in the scene. But it is a useful primary source which a historian can use either on its own, or in conjunction with other sources, such as an onlooker's written description of the same type of scene.

The photograph above shows Skye crofters in the 1880s planting potatoes, a staple of the islanders' diet. The men are using the traditional foot plough or 'caschrom', and the women are fertilizing the ground with seaweed. This shows that farming on the island was still unmechanised and highly labour intensive. We can see houses in the background, and the style of clothes worn by the crofters.

Some photographs, like those of the demonstrators in the square in Petrograd in 1917 (page 97), or the air raid on Pearl Harbor in December 1941 (page 100), bring to life a major crisis or world event. It is one thing to read Nikolai Sukhanov's written account of the demonstration in Petrograd (page 10), but the photograph on page 97 gives it a new dimension, and helps us to see for ourselves the scale of the challenge which faced the Czar and his officials.

A District Commissioner hears the case against a Sudanese offender at a local court in the Sudan in 1952. Which is the District Commissioner? Which is the offender? How does this scene differ from one in Britain when an offender is brought to court? Do you think it is true that we gave our colonies the same system of justice as in Britain?

Photographs can also be used as sources of information from which we can deduce many other facts about the past. The photograph of the District Commissioner in the Sudan in 1952 helps us to understand how Britain exercised control over a huge colonial Empire by employing local people to maintain law and order. The primitive buildings betray the basic poverty of the area – hence the need to hold the court out of doors despite the hot tropical sun. Note the immaculate white tropical kit of the District Commissioner, contrasted with the clothes of the Sudanese people present at the court hearing.

If you have no precise date for a photograph it is always possible to estimate its date by examining the style of clothes worn by the people in the photograph and also from other pictorial clues, such as makes and types of cars, trams, buses, aeroplanes, and ships.

However, there are some serious drawbacks to the use of photographs as historical evidence. Although a photograph helps you to become an eyewitness to history, it is by no means certain that what you see is a fair representation of reality itself. Photographers select the viewpoints for their photographs. They decide what the photograph will show, *not* the camera! The photograph of the District Commissioner in the Sudan may or may not be typical of similar local outdoor courts throughout the British Empire. Questions like this can only be answered by studying other photographs and by comparing them with pictures and written accounts.

Bear in mind, too, that the camera can also lie. Photographs are sometimes altered to improve the appearance of the people shown in the pictures or to block out something which spoils the view. Some photographs have even been deliberately faked. In *The Independent* for 3 December 1987, Oliver Knox revealed that his cousin

> was in 1964 briefly Chancellor of the Exchequer. Very briefly indeed. The official photograph of the full Cabinet about to be taken, Reginald Maudling was urgently summoned away; and Tony in No. 11 on Treasury business, was press-ganged into deputising – to be decapitated of course when the photograph was printed.

In dictatorships, skilled darkroom assistants have sometimes altered old photographs in order to eliminate a later enemy of the state shown in the earlier photograph to be standing far too close to the Dictator! As you saw on page 30, a poor or unflattering photograph can be printed in a newspaper to try to turn public opinion against a politician.

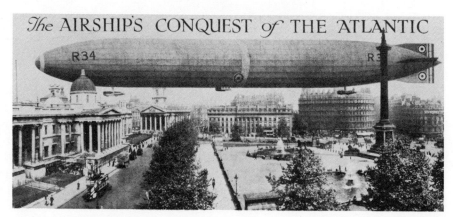

The AIRSHIP'S CONQUEST of THE ATLANTIC

This photograph showing the immense size of the R34 airship was printed in The Graphic *on 12 July 1919. How do you think the photograph was taken?*

Checklist — Photographs

1   *What does the photograph show? What does it tell us about the past?*

2   *When and where was the photograph taken? If no date is given use clues to estimate the date.*

3   *Why was the photograph taken? Is there any reason to think the photographer chose a viewpoint or a subject to make us feel in a certain way about the event or people depicted?*

4   *Is there any sign that the people in the photograph are posing for the photographer? Were they aware of the camera? Does this make any difference to the value of the photograph?*

5   *Is there any reason to think that the photograph is not a typical example of what it appears to show? Is there any reason to think that it may have been altered in any way?*

Going through the Checklist

SOURCE A

Photograph showing demonstrators in the square in front of St Isaac's Cathedral in Petrograd during the Russian Revolution in 1917

1 *What does the photograph show? What does it tell us about the past?*

It shows thousands of demonstrators completely packing one of the main squares in Petrograd during the Russian Revolution in 1917 (see page 10). The caption to the photograph does not say whether this was in March, when the Czar was overthrown, or in November, when Lenin and the Bolsheviks seized power. However, the people in the crowd are waving their hats and cheering the person addressing them from a plinth to the left of the statue of the horseman in the centre of the photograph. There are also men in uniform mingling with the crowd. Many Russian soldiers and policemen refused to take action against the demonstrators in the March revolution. The banners look like those carried by the trade unionists and striking workers who protested against bread shortages and against the War in March 1917. But this is not conclusive evidence, many workers also demonstrated in November.

2 *When and where was the photograph taken?*

Probably in March 1917 in Petrograd (now Leningrad) but it could have been in November.

3 *Why was the photograph taken? Is there any reason to think the photographer chose a viewpoint or a subject to make us feel in a certain way about the event or people depicted?*

No – apart from a desire to show the immense size of the crowds of demonstrators. Judging by the high viewpoint above the crowd, the photographer may have been standing on the plinth of another statue in order to take the photograph.

4 *Is there any sign that the people in the photograph are posing for the photographer? Were they aware of the camera?*

Crowds of this size do not pose for photographers. Almost all are engrossed by the stirring events of the day. Only one or two people can be seen looking towards the camera.

5 *Is there any reason to think that the photograph is not a typical example of what it appears to show? Is there any reason to think that it may have been altered in any way?*

No.

SOURCE B

Photograph showing Russian and American soldiers meeting at Torgau on the Elbe in April 1945

1 *What does the photograph show? What does it tell us about the past?*

It shows American soldiers on the left and Russian soldiers on the right shaking hands. The photograph shows clearly that forward units of the two great Allied armies – the Red Army from the East and Eisenhower's Army from the West – had completely encircled Germany. It was only a matter of days before Germany was defeated.

2 *When and where was the photograph taken?*

On or about 27 April 1945 at Torgau (near Leipzig) on the river Elbe in what is now East Germany.

3 *Why was the photograph taken? Is there any reason to think the photographer chose a viewpoint or a subject to make us feel in a certain way about the event or people depicted?*

The photograph was obviously taken to symbolise the linking up of the two great Allied armies. It gives every indication of having been carefully posed to enable the photographer to create an interesting and striking picture. After fighting their way across Europe, however, you might have expected these soldiers, especially the Russians, to embrace each other in the style of soccer players after a goal has been scored! Instead they shake hands! Did the photographer want us to feel a slight chill between the two armies?

4 *Is there any sign that the people in the photograph are posing for the photographer? Were they aware of the camera?*

What do you think?

5 *Is there any reason to think that the photograph is not a typical example of what it appears to show? Is there any reason to think that it may have been altered in any way?*

No.

EXERCISES AND ACTIVITIES

1 *Use the checklist on page 96 to help you study the two photographs printed on page 100.*

2 *Both photographs have been reprinted many times. Why? What was their value to the Americans as propaganda in the war against the Japanese?*

3 *What is the value of these photographs, if any, to the historian of the Second World War?*

Pearl Harbor, 7 December 1941

On the summit of Mount Suribachi on the Pacific island of Iwo Jima, 23 February 1945

4 *The next two photographs contrast housing in nineteenth century Glasgow and on the Isle of Eriskay in the mid-twentieth century. Use the checklist on page 96 to check out these photographs.*

A Glasgow close

Thatching on the Isle of Eriskay

5 *The photograph below shows islanders returning to Vatersay after Sunday service at Castlebay, around 1947. What does it reveal about the islanders' way of life and attitudes? What can you say about their clothes?*

EVIDENCE IN SOUND AND ON FILM

The first sound recordings were made by Thomas Alva Edison in 1877. The first moving films were made in the 1890s. These two great inventions provided historians with important new sources of evidence. Since they are not in printed form, however, their value in the study of history has not always been appreciated. Only since the coming of television has effective use been made of old film for the benefit of the general public. As a result people can now see movie film of the funeral of Queen Victoria in 1901 or watch the coronation of Queen Elizabeth II in 1953. Old movie films enable us to see or hear some of the events of history as they happened.

The main drawback to the use of movie film is that it can be easily edited (altered) to show whatever the film editor wants us to see. Lengths of movie film can be cut out and then stuck back together in a different order. It is very easy to assume that because the images are moving in a documentary film we are actually seeing events in sequence exactly as they happened at the time. In many cases you are, but you cannot be certain of this! Movie film has been one of the most powerful weapons used by people involved in propaganda (as in Nazi Germany) and in advertising (see also pages 69–72).

On pages 24–26 you saw evidence relating to the tragic death of Emily Wilding Davison after the Epsom Derby on 4 June 1913. A movie film was made of the race and shown at the Palace Theatre in London. This is how a journalist on *The Times* described the film when he saw it shown for the first time on Derby night, 1913.

The tragic incident at the 1913 Derby

A CINEMATOGRAPH VIEW

The scene at Tattenham Corner was shown on the cinematograph at the Palace Theatre last night. Viewed from a point opposite Tattenham Corner the vast crowd was seen with every head turned in the direction from which the horses were coming. A moment later a bunch, so closely packed that it is scarcely possible to distinguish one horse from another, passed at a great pace. There is a pause for a moment, and suddenly a woman is seen to spring forward from behind the white rails, but as she sets foot upon the course two horses come by. There is a flicker and a flash of white, the woman is prostrate on the turf and a jockey is flung head foremost from his mount and lies in a huddled heap a dozen yards from the woman. A moment more and the remaining horses have passed, but the jockey and the woman lie still and silent, and then the great crowd, moved by a common impulse, closes round them.

The Times, Thursday, 5 June 1913

As it happens, we can see this film ourselves, since the clip of film described in this report has been shown several times on television. It has also been included in at least one schools' television broadcast.

Immediately after the incident, some eyewitnesses said that Emily Wilding Davison deliberately tried to stop the race but others thought that she had mistakenly assumed the race was over and was trying to get to the other side of the racecourse. To the eyewitnesses at Epsom, glued to the race, the incident, which was over in a flash, came as a complete and unexpected shock. It was unthinkable that anyone would actually want to run on to the track during the race. Not surprisingly, they had different versions of what happened in the midst of the confusion.

The modern viewer of this movie film when seen on a video recorder has no such excuse for not knowing exactly what happened! Slow motion and the rewind button can be used to get an instant replay of history! In other words you can be an eyewitness to an important historical event, but with the added advantage of being able to repeat the film over and over again until you think you know for sure what happened.

Almost every historian who has ever described this event in print (including the author until he saw the video recording of a schools broadcast!) is on record as saying that Emily Wilding Davison 'threw herself under the King's horse'. This is because everyone later assumed that this is what must have happened, since she was a suffragette and presumably wanted to bring the cause of the suffragettes to the notice of the world. What better way to do this than by throwing herself in front of the King's horse to disrupt the most famous horse race in the world?

Here, instead, is a modern 'eyewitness' account of the 1913 Derby written after watching about a dozen replays of this incident on a video recorder.

Emily Wilding Davison can be seen clearly ducking under the barrier after the leading horses have passed. She stands upright in the middle of the racecourse, facing the remaining horses in the race. Her arms appear to be stretched outwards. At no time does she fling herself under the hooves of a horse. She seems bewildered, at first, trying to grab at the reins of three horses all close together and passing her far too quickly for her to have any chance of stopping them. Then there is a short gap in the field. It is enough to give her the chance to position herself and reach up to the next horse as it races towards her. She grabs at the reins again but is knocked down and the horse and the jockey also fall. Two other horses ride past as they lie on the ground.

In other words, the 'cinematograph film' proves conclusively that:

- Emily Wilding Davison did not throw herself under the hooves of the King's horse. Far from it. She was standing upright all the time and her only motion when the horse approached was to reach up with her hands towards the reins.
- It was sheer chance that the horse that knocked her down was Anmer, the King's horse. In fact, she tried to stop the earlier horses as soon as she stepped on to the race track.
- Anmer was third from last at Tattenham Corner. It was *not* leading the field, nor was it the last horse in the race. This corrects the misleading statements in Sources A (page 24) and D (page 25).

These may seem trivial points but they do have some importance to the history of the suffragette movement. In the first place they suggest that Emily Davison did not really set out to become a martyr at all although she did want to stop or disrupt the race. In fact she gives every impression of having been taken aback by the speed of the horses. So perhaps she was not quite the heroine and martyr portrayed by the suffragettes in their subsequent literature. Equally she was not the 'half demented' woman depicted by many commentators and historians both at the time and since.

EXERCISES AND ACTIVITIES

Look closely at clips of old newsreel film on a video recorder or whenever an old documentary film is shown on schools television. Use your eyes and ears to note carefully what happens. Record your observations as an eyewitness would have done had he or she been a witness to the same event.

If possible take the opportunity to view the film of the 1913 Derby. Write your own 'eyewitness' account of the incident and compare it with those printed above.

FACTS FROM STATISTICS

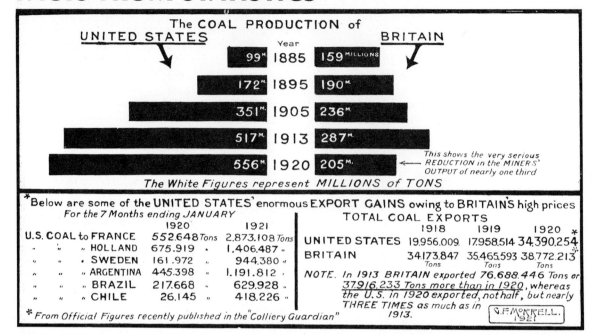

The COAL PRODUCTION of
UNITED STATES — Year — BRITAIN

UNITED STATES	Year	BRITAIN
99ᴹ	1885	159 MILLIONS
172ᴹ	1895	190ᴹ
351ᴹ	1905	236ᴹ
517ᴹ	1913	287ᴹ
556ᴹ	1920	205ᴹ

← This shows the very serious REDUCTION in the MINERS' OUTPUT of nearly one third

The White Figures represent MILLIONS of TONS

*Below are some of the UNITED STATES' enormous EXPORT GAINS owing to BRITAIN'S high prices
For the 7 Months ending JANUARY

U.S. COAL to	1920	1921
FRANCE	552.648 Tons	2.873.108 Tons
" " " HOLLAND	675.919 "	1.406.487 "
" " • SWEDEN	161.972 "	944.380 "
" " " ARGENTINA	445.398 "	1.191.812 "
" " " BRAZIL	217.668 "	629.928 "
" " " CHILE	26.145 "	418.226 "

* From Official Figures recently published in the "Colliery Guardian"

TOTAL COAL EXPORTS

	1918	1919	1920 *
UNITED STATES	19.956.009	17.958.514	34.390.254
BRITAIN	34.173.847	35.465.593	38.772.213
	Tons	Tons	Tons

NOTE. In 1913 BRITAIN exported 76.688.446 Tons or 37.916.233 Tons more than in 1920, whereas the U.S. in 1920 exported, not half, but nearly THREE TIMES as much as in 1913.

T.F. MORRELL. 1921

Why do you think this graph and the statistics underneath were published in The Graphic *on 14 May 1921 at the time of a coal miners' strike? What were these statistics designed to show? How did they affect two of the main developments of the 1920s – the 'Boom and Bust' years in the United States and the General Strike in Great Britain?*

Statistics are an important source of information for the historian. The most important sources of statistics in British history are the official census reports which have been published every ten years since the first Census in 1801. Official statistics of wartime casualties, army recruitment, agricultural and industrial production, length of railway line, numbers of people unemployed, and countless other statistics have also been published. Statistics like these are invaluable since they help us to measure the effect of war, the progress or decline of industries, and the growth or decline of towns.

But there are problems. Some statistics can mislead. They may have been collected or counted in circumstances which led to inaccuracies. The first census reports were compiled from census returns, completed by householders, many of whom were illiterate. Sometimes the statistics are biased. They may be incomplete.

Many printed statistics, like opinion polls, are based on samples, instead of being complete surveys. Statistics for 1930 tell us about 1930. These may or may not be typical of the 1930s as a whole. Statistics for London tell us about London, not about the rest of Britain. Unfortunately, you will rarely have the chance to check for yourself when, how, why and where the statistics were collected and whether they are reliable.

This is why it is best to treat all statistics with a certain amount of caution and to use them as a guide rather than as proof. In particular, beware of believing statistics just because they back up your own or other people's arguments!

Checklist — **Statistics**

1   When and how were the statistics collected? Who collected them? Were they in a position to collect accurate or reliable statistics? Can we be certain they are not guesses, estimates, approximations, or even lies?

2   Is it likely that someone else working in exactly the same way would collect the same statistics? If not, why not?

3   Are the statistics complete or only a sample of all the possible statistics which could have been recorded?

4   Who selected the statistics for use and how were they chosen?

5   What do the statistics tell you about the past? What do they prove? If they are quoted to back up a statement do they really support the conclusions drawn from them by the writer?

6   Are the statistics used to support a statement which may be biased or prejudiced?

7   If averages are used do they mean anything? See if you can find out how they were calculated.

Going through the Checklist

This German grocer needed a tea chest to hold the day's takings in 1923!

The statistics printed below show the decline in the value of the German paper mark compared with the value of gold in the period between January 1919 and November 1923. A gold mark was worth 1.97 paper marks in January 1919. A year later it was worth 19.86 paper marks. In other words, the value of the paper mark fell to only a tenth of its former value in the course of twelve months. Ten times as much paper money was needed to buy the same amount of gold in January 1920 as in January 1919. This was an inflation rate of about 1000 per cent.

	1919	1920	1921	1922	1923
January	1.97	19.86	14.40	47.89	1167
February	2.18	23.93	14.97	54.17	3405
March	2.48	17.38	14.87	72.62	4994
April	3.04	13.63	15.74	67.38	7096
May	3.09	8.87	15.06	65.95	16 550
June	3.33	9.17	17.89	89.17	36 790
July	3.59	10.12	19.20	159.52	261 900
August	4.60	11.85	20.56	410.71	2 453 000
September	5.81	14.82	27.50	392.86	38 100 000
October	6.50	18.21	42.98	1071.00	17 261 000 000
November	9.29	16.85	58.33	1821.00	1 000 000 000 000
December	11.47	17.47	43.81	1750.00	

Heinz Huber and Artur Muller, *Das Dritte Reich*, Verlag Kurt Desch, 1964

1　*When and how were the statistics collected? Who collected them?*

Like most published statistics we have little information on this. They may have been calculated by a German bank or by a Government department.

2　*Is it likely that someone else working in exactly the same way would collect the same statistics?*

No. The sweeping changes from month to month in 1922–3 must mean that different figures would have been shown had the statistics been collected on the 1st, 15th, or 30th of each month, or as an average of each month.

3　*Are the statistics complete or only a sample of all the possible statistics which could have been recorded?*

They are only a sample since the statistics could have been recorded week by week or even day by day.

4 *Who selected the statistics for use and how were they chosen?*

No information — but we can only assume that the statistics were collected in the same way each month.

5 *What do the statistics tell you about the past? What do they prove? If they are quoted to back up a statement do they really support the conclusions drawn from them by the writer?*

The statistics show that inflation was a serious problem in Germany even in 1919; between January 1919 and January 1920 the mark dropped to a tenth of its former value. By November 1923, it had become virtually worthless.

6 *Are the statistics used to support any statement which may be biased or prejudiced?*

No.

EXERCISES AND ACTIVITIES

1 *Draw graphs to show the rise and fall of the German mark:*
(a) In the three years from 1919 to 1921, (b) in 1922, (c) in 1923,
(d) for all five years.
What do you notice after studying the graphs you have drawn? Did the value of the mark decline at a steady rate? Did it always fall in value throughout the entire period of almost five years? In which year was the value of the mark most erratic? Write a paragraph describing the problem of inflation in Germany in the five years before December 1923.

In 1910 Dr Newman, the Chief Medical Officer of the Board of Education, published a report on the first official survey of the health of children in Britain's public elementary schools, following the passing of the Health Inspection Act by the Liberal government of 1907. This is how *The Times* (30 November 1910) summed up his findings.

> The Report throws an appalling light upon the absolute amount of disease from which the children now at school are suffering . . . Ten per cent suffer from defective sight, three to five per cent from defective hearing, eight per cent from adenoid growths obstructive of proper breathing, twenty to forty per cent from unclean heads, and about one per cent from ringworm, tuberculosis, and heart disease.

2 *Go through the checklist for statistics on page 107.*

3 *Who do you think collected these statistics in the first place? Is there any chance that they were mistaken? Show the statistics as a graph.*

4 *Suggest reasons which might account for these 'appalling' figures. Why do you think* The Times *was surprised by these figures?*

Working as a Historian

SIMILARITIES AND DIFFERENCES

Similarity does not mean 'the same'. It means that things are alike in certain respects but not identical. This is an important difference. Two mill towns may look alike to an outsider but they may be very different places to the people who actually live there.

In fact every historical event is unique. There is nothing quite like it. This is why it is often much easier to detect differences than it is to find similarities. Nevertheless there are patterns in history. A revolution in one country may be followed by similar revolutions in neighbouring countries.

If you are asked to look for similarities and differences in history you may be asked to compare two or three written extracts or a number of pictures or photographs. You will need to pick out the important things that matter, not the minor details. If you jot down the main similarities and differences first of all, you can use these lists later on to help plan your essay.

EXERCISES AND ACTIVITIES

Study Sources A, B, C, D and the photographs. They show how people greeted the outbreak of the First World War in London and Berlin.

SOURCE A

A JOURNALIST IN LONDON

AUG: (Piccadilly Hotel) Was awakened by loud noises. Great crowds are parading the streets, exulting in the anticipation of war. This mafficking [rejoicing] for such universal tragedy makes me feel sad, and I am unable to sleep. Wasn't it Walpole who said: 'Yes! they are ringing their bells now; soon they will be wringing their hands!'? ... I cannot sleep. They are going mad. Have they no imagination? They say war with Germany is inevitable. Possibly so – but why jubilate [rejoice] – how *can* they? ... Can they not realize what war really means, these mad maffickers – what it means to women as well as men?

The Private Diaries of Sydney Moseley, Max Parrish, 1960

SOURCE B

A LONDON NEWSPAPER

A lady came out of the Palace, and announced that war had been declared. This was received with tremendous cheering, which grew into a deafening roar when King George, Queen Mary and the Prince of Wales appeared on the balcony shortly after eleven o'clock.

They looked down upon an extraordinary scene – a dense mass of excited people, many of whom had clambered on to the Victoria

Memorial. As if by general accord, the cheers gave way to the singing of the National Anthem, which was taken up lustily by the whole throng.

For fully five minutes the Royal Party remained on the balcony. They retired amidst a perfect storm of cheering, and although the crowd subsequently began to melt away, thousands remained. They grew gradually less demonstrative, and it was noticeable that the news of the actual state of war had a sobering effect on many. Mafficking gave way to distinct seriousness.

Daily News and Leader, 5 August 1914

*Crowds outside
Buckingham Palace.
London, August 1914*

*Crowds in the Unter
den Linden. Berlin,
August 1914*

SOURCE C

A BRITISH JOURNALIST IN BERLIN

For two days I waited and watched. Up and down the wide road of Unter den Linden crowds paced incessantly by day and night singing the German war songs: 'Was blasen die Trompeten?' [Who blows the trumpet?] which is the finest; 'Deutschland, Deutschland ueber Alles,' [Germany, Germany above all] which comes next, and 'Die Wacht am Rhein,' [The Watch on the Rhine] which was the most popular... Sometimes the Kaiser in full uniform swept along in his fine motor... Cheered he was certainly, but everyone believed or knew that the Kaiser himself had never wished for war... The most mighty storm of cheering was reserved for the Crown Prince, known to be at variance with his father in longing to test his imagined genius on the field. Him the people cheered, for they had never known war.

Henry W. Nevinson, *More Changes, More Chances*,
James Nisbet, 1925

SOURCE D

A BRITISH WOMAN IN BERLIN

BERLIN, August 9th, 1914.
The excitement and enthusiasm all over the city are enormous.
The Kaiser is the most adored man of the moment, and during a
great speech he delivered the other day on the balcony of the
castle, in spite of the people standing densely thronged together,
the silence was so great that one might have heard a pin fall.
Certainly the whole nation are backing him this time, and if he has
been criticized for his actions in the past, this war-cry is making
him the most popular man in Germany.

Evelyn, Princess Blücher, *An English Wife in Berlin*,
Constable, 1921
[She and her German husband had been living in
England but returned to Germany on 6 August 1914.]

1   *Use the master checklist on page 54 to check out these sources first of
all. Are they primary sources? Are they eyewitness accounts? Which parts
of these extracts are facts and which are opinions?*

2   *What were the similarities and differences between Berlin and London in
the way in which people greeted the war? How do you account for the
similarities? Is that how people always greet a declaration of war?*

3   *Do any of the writers appear to be biased or prejudiced? The descriptions
of Berlin were written by people who were British not German. Is there
any sign that this may have affected the way in which they described the
reactions of the Germans to the war?*

4   *Do the photographs support or contradict the written sources? In what
ways are these photographs similar?*

5   *Do the written sources support or contradict each other?*

6   *Do you think you have enough information to be able to say how
people, in general, greeted the outbreak of war in August 1914?*

The accounts which follow also describe scenes at the outbreak of the
First World War but in Buxton, a small English country town (Source E)
and in a village near the French fishing port and holiday resort of Morlaix
in Brittany (Source F).

SOURCE E

BUXTON, ENGLAND

Wednesday, August 5th
The town was quite quiet when we went down, though groups of
people were standing about talking & one or two Territorials [part-
time soldiers] were passing through the streets. Several Territorials
& one or two Reservists were going off by train this morning &

there was a small crowd on the station seeing them off. Close by us a Reservist got into a carriage & his father & a girl, probably his wife, came to say goodbye. The girl was crying but they were all quite calm . . . Though excitement & suspense are wearing, I felt I simply could not rest but must go on wandering about.

Vera Brittain, *Chronicle of Youth*, Victor Gollancz, 1981

SOURCE F

A BRETON VILLAGE NEAR MORLAIX, FRANCE

It was Saturday afternoon [2nd August]. Everybody was waiting in the streets. The beach was empty. At midday the news had already gone round that the order for mobilization would arrive any moment. I went once more to the post office to enquire . . .

About half-past two the clerk of the Mairie arrived on a bicycle, with ceaseless bell-ringing, from the direction of Morlaix. He was hugging a black portfolio under his arm. The mobilization order.

> [Mobilization meant that many of the men in the town would be called up immediately to serve in the French army in case war broke out against Germany. It did – the next day – 3 August].

At three o'clock the tocsin [alarm] shrieked. The senseless clanging of the village church bell was a worthy heralding of the world's gloomy change . . .

Old women in black with white head-dresses came hurrying. Suddenly they were all over the space round the platform which had been set up in front of the church, like big, white-crested, black birds. Then the men, as many of them as were at home, arrived in their Sunday clothes.

The holiday-makers silently made way for the assembling villagers. They had first right to hear the news.

In deathly silence the mayor read out the order for general mobilization.

Then petrified dumbness. Not a voice applauded. Someone sobbed, once, and the crowd stirred, and everyone went their various ways home.

Aladar Kuncz, *Black Monastery*, Chatto & Windus

5 Use the master checklist on page 54 to check out Sources E and F. Are they primary sources? Are they eyewitness reports? Which parts of these extracts appear to be facts and which are opinions?

6 Make a list of the ways in which the events depicted in these two extracts are similar to each other and how they differ from Sources A to D.

7 Which of the six extracts do you think you would pick if you had to choose one to read out at a Remembrance Day ceremony?

SOURCE G

Cover of the German
magazine Jugend, *issue*
no. 3 published in
1916

SOURCE H

TO THE GLORY OF FRANCE.

Cartoon in Punch *in*
March 1916
commemorating the
epic battle at Verdun
in which over 200,000
French soldiers were
killed

8 *What are the similarities and differences between Sources G and H?*

9 *What is the link between Source G and Source C?*

10 *How did the artist who drew Source G expect the German people to react to his picture? How did the Punch artist expect people in Britain to react?*

11 What was the point of the two cartoons below? Why were they drawn?

12 What are the similarities between these two cartoons?

Russian propaganda cartoon in 1919 showing the United States controlling the commanders of the three main White Armies (Denikin, Kolchak, and Kudenich). The White Armies were fighting the Red Army in the Russian Civil War. You can see a reference to the White Armies in the extract printed on page 33.

German propaganda cartoon from the Second World War – ENTENTE CORDIALE – showing Churchill (left), Stalin (centre) and Roosevelt (right)

HOW THINGS CHANGE

28 July 1789: I am sure I need not tell you how much I have rejoiced at the Revolution which has taken place. I think of nothing else, and please myself with endeavouring to guess at some of the important consequences which must follow throughout Europe.

10 September 1792: How could we ever be so deceived in the character of the French nation as to think them capable of liberty! Wretches, who, after all their professions and boasts about liberty, and patriotism, and courage, and dying, and after taking oath after oath, at the very moment when their country is invaded and the enemy is marching through it unresisted, employ whole days in murdering women, and priests, and prisoners!

Letters from Sir Samuel Romilly to Etienne Dumont

These letters show how rapidly people change their attitudes to great events. How and why things change is of great interest to historians. Sometimes the changes are abrupt and clear cut, such as the sudden change in policy which happens when a revolutionary government seizes power. Changes of equal or greater significance in the lives of ordinary people also take place but often slowly over periods of many years.

Despite these changes many things, such as people's attitudes, customs and traditions, often remain much the same. This is called *continuity*. Change and continuity can both be identified when you make comparisons over a period of time.

Checklist — Change

Use these checkpoints if you are asked to identify changes which may have taken place.

1   *What was the nature of the change? Was it part of a much bigger change?*

2   *Was it an important and significant change? Did it affect everybody and almost every activity, like the coming of the railway, motor car and telephone? Or did it affect just a section of the community, such as the effect of the means test in the 1930s on the unemployed?*

3   *Who or what benefited from the change? Who or what suffered from the change?*

4   *Did the change take place suddenly, rapidly, steadily, slowly, jerkily, or imperceptibly?*

5   *Did the change affect people mainly because of its political effects, such as its effect on relations with other countries? Or because of its social and economic effects, such as on health or on industry?*

Going through the Checklist

BERLIN

November 8, 1918

I wonder what the result of the meeting of the delegates for an armistice today will be? . . . Every one expects that France will take her fill of revenge and make terms as hard as she can. Poor Germany is not in a position to resist any humiliation; she is completely exhausted.

Evening, November 9, 1918

Gebhardt and I were sitting quietly reading our papers, when at about two o'clock a perfect avalanche of humanity began to stream by our windows, walking quietly enough, many of them carrying red flags . . .

Our butler came in to announce that the Kaiser had abdicated. Tears came into both our eyes as we grasped the momentousness of the hour . . . But it was not time to mourn for the individual, and our attention was soon fixed on what was passing outside our windows. There, evidently no one sorrowed at the loss of an emperor. There could hardly have been a greater air of rejoicing had Germany gained a great victory. More and more people came hurrying by, thousands of them densely packed together – men, women, soldiers, sailors . . .

Sunday morning, November 10, 1918

After we had all separated for the night, I lay awake, very tired. We were constantly disturbed by the sound of stray rifle-shots, and the feeling of uncertainty as to what was going on out there in the darkness of the huge city made sleep impossible . . .

Princess Taxis rang us up to say that the new Socialist Chancellor, Ebert, has already threatened to resign as he cannot hold the people . . . Amongst the aristocracy the grief at the breakdown of their country, more than at the personal fall of the Kaiser, is quite heart-rending to see. I have seen some of our friends, strong men, sit down and sob at the news, whilst others seemed to shrink to half their size and were struck dumb with pain.

Evelyn, Princess Blücher, *An English Wife in Berlin*,
Constable, 1921

Compare the extract above with the same writer's description of Berlin and the Kaiser at the start of the war only four years earlier (Source D on page 112).

1   *What was the nature of the change? Was it part of a much bigger change?*

It was a catastrophic change. Germany was exhausted; the armistice was about to be signed; the abdication of the Kaiser had brought to an end the Prussian monarchy and the German Empire. Germany was now a socialist republic. There was a very real possibility of a communist revolution, following the example of the Bolsheviks in Russia a year earlier.

2   *Was it an important and significant change? Did it affect everybody and almost every activity, or just a section of the community?*

Obviously it was an important and significant change, affecting everybody living in Germany. The autocratic rule of the Kaiser was at an end. No one knew what sort of government would take its place. The Princess Blücher was most disturbed at the uncertain future which lay ahead.

3   *Who or what benefited from the change? Who or what suffered from the change?*

The ordinary people, soldiers, sailors, strikers obviously thought that they would benefit. The aristocracy assumed that they would suffer and that their world had come to an end. The Princess Blücher described their 'grief at the breakdown of their country' and said that their reaction was

> quite heart-rending to see. I have seen some of our friends, strong men, sit down and sob at the news, whilst others seemed to shrink to half their size and were struck dumb with pain.

4   *Did the change take place suddenly, rapidly, steadily, slowly, jerkily, or imperceptibly?*

Suddenly with the collapse of the German war effort. The abdication of the Kaiser obviously came as a great shock – 'Tears came into both our eyes as we grasped the momentousness of the hour'.

5   *Did the change affect people mainly because of its political effects? Or because of its social and economic effects?*

Mainly because of its political effects at the time. It was too early to say what the social and economic effects would be.

EXERCISES AND ACTIVITIES

This Russian propaganda comic strip was published in *The Graphic* on 29 May 1920, less than three years after the start of the Bolshevik Revolution in Russia in November 1917.

PETER WORKED HARD
ON HIS CORNFIELD

WHILE VASSILY WAS
DRUNK BOTH NIGHT
AND DAY

Just at this time there fell upon Russia a great misfortune – the régime of the Soviet.

A SOVIET ORATOR
ARRIVED ON THE
SCENE

AND FOR VASSILY
THERE CAME A HIGH
OLD TIME

BUT PETER WAS VERY
HARDLY DEALT WITH

When a Leninite orator came down the drunken and ragged Vassily was the most enthusiastic of those present at the meeting, and was rewarded by being the first to receive authority over the village ... Vassily proclaimed the socialisation of property, and carried off all poor Peter's belongings.

*AND THIS IS WHAT HAPPENED TO THE VILLAGE AFTER
A MONTH OF THE BOLSHEVIK REGIME*

The result was that while some of the inhabitants deserted the
village with their children, others lay in the cold grey earth. It was
decreed that whoever had worked all his life with industrious
hands was a harmful man. The cattle died and only the Soviet
Committee and the dogs had enough to eat. Thus did the
Bolshevik Vassily rule. While these pictures may be exaggerated,
the story told in words is not; it is an accurate description of what
has been happening all over Russia since the country had the
tragic misfortune to fall under the tyranny of its new rulers. The
people live under a perpetual Reign of Terror without parallel in
Russian history. Murder stalks abroad in the land. Outrages are
committed everywhere. The industrial life of the great nation has
been paralysed. Famine has been added to the horrors of the
people. Nothing is deemed sacred by the authors of this prolonged
orgy of fiendish misrule.

The Graphic, 29 May 1920

1 *Examine this propaganda strip with the aid of the checklist for bias and
   prejudice on page 31. In particular, examine the way in which it was used
   by The Graphic.*

2 *What changes did the Bolshevik Revolution have on Russia according to
   the authors of this propaganda strip? Use the checklist printed on page
   116 to examine these changes.*

3 *Find out what really happened to agriculture in Russia in the first three
   years under communism. Was there any truth whatsoever in the
   propaganda strip? Was it 'an accurate description of what has been
   happening all over Russia since the country had the tragic misfortune to
   fall under the tyranny of its new rulers'?*

IMAGING THE PAST

Trying to imagine what it was like to live in the past is called historical *empathy*. It is a way of trying to understand why people behaved in the past in the way they did. Instead of judging their actions by our own standards we look at events and happenings through the eyes of the people living at that time.

Really understanding what happened in the past will only come about if you can set aside your own ideas and background and picture yourself in the past. How would you have behaved then? A good way of imagining yourself in the past is to think of everything in the present tense! What are your thoughts as you wait for the command 'to go over the top' at the battle of the Somme in 1916? What will you do if a Prussian officer takes over your house in Paris as a billet for his troops? Is it safe to walk near the Bastille at night?

Another way of getting a vivid picture of what it was really like to live in the past is to read accounts and stories which tell you how people spoke and how they behaved. Look closely at old pictures and especially at old photographs. When you see a photograph of a Victorian or an Edwardian town, for instance, try to imagine what it would have been like to be there when the photographer took the picture.

EXERCISES AND ACTIVITIES

The Highland Clearances

In the nineteenth century, Highland landlords transformed the system of agriculture on their estates by introducing sheep in large numbers. This destroyed the simple subsistence farms of their tenants. In the Highland clearances, the Scottish Highlands lost much of their population, as thousands of tenants were evicted or left voluntarily, to emigrate to north America, or to work in the mills and shipyards and to live in the slums of Glasgow.

Look at the following sources on the Highland clearances (pages 122–125), and answer the questions on page 125.

SOURCE A

Crofters grinding oatmeal, 1880s

SOURCE B

A large pot of potatoes hung suspended over the fire, under a dense ceiling of smoke; and he hospitably invited us to wait supper, which as our dinner had consisted of but a piece of dry oaten cake, we willingly did. Our host regretted he had no fish to offer us; rough weather had kept him from the sea, and he had just exhausted his previous supply; as for bread, he had used up the last of his grain crop a little after Christmas, and he had been living, with his family, on potatoes, with fish when he could get them, ever since.

Hugh Miller, *My Schools and Schoolmasters*, 1852, Edinburgh

SOURCE C

It is not too much to say that many of the swine in England are better fed and better housed than are the poor of this island.

Report of the Highland Emigration Society, 1853

SOURCE D

Under sheep, the Highland would be six, if not ten times more valuable than under cattle, if the proper breeds were introduced.

Sir John Sinclair, *General View of Agriculture in the Northern Counties*, 1795, Appendix, p. 41

SOURCE E

The greater part of those who were dispossessed of their farms betook themselves to a seafaring life, or settled in the populous towns upon the Clyde; and thus were taken from a situation where they contributed nothing to the wealth, and very little to the support or defence of the state, to situations in which their labour is of the greatest possible utility, where they have an easy opportunity also of training up their children to be useful and valuable members of society.

Sir John Sinclair, *An Account of the Systems of Husbandry adopted in the more improved Districts of Scotland*, 1814

SOURCE F

THE SUTHERLAND CLEARANCE, 1819

To my poor and defenceless flock the dark hour of trial came at last in right earnest. It was in the month of April, that they were all, man, woman, and child, from the heights of Farr to the mouth of Naver, on one day, to quit their tenements, and go – many of them knew not whither. For a few, some miserable patches of ground along the shore were doled out as lots, with aught in the shape of the poorest hut to shelter them. . . .

The middle of the week brought on the day of the Strathnaver Clearance. Mr Sellar, accompanied by the Fiscal, and escorted by a strong body of constables, sheriff-officers and others, commenced work. . . . Their plan of operations was to clear the cottages of their inmates, giving them about half-an-hour to pack up and carry off their furniture, and then set the cottages on fire. To this plan they ruthlessly adhered, without the slightest regard to any obstacle that might arise. . . .

On the week immediately ensuing I passed through the scene of the campaign of burning. The spectacle presented was hideous and ghastly! ... The sooty rafters of the cottages, as they were being consumed, filled the air with a heavy and most offensive odour.

Rev D. Sage, *Memorabilia Domestica*, 1889

SOURCE G

Eviction of Highlanders

SOURCE H

I am told that the island is over-peopled and my farms filled with a numerous set of poor tenants and cottars. I wish to relieve the farms of these people, and as I do not want to distress them I will help them to settle in a fishing village which I mean to set up in a suitable spot on the island.

Orders of the Duke of Argyll to his factor on the island of Tiree, 1771

SOURCE I

A number of crofters were ejected last year from the estate of Lochshiel and were assisted to emigrate to Canada. A few of them have written to their friends at home and given so favourable an account of the land of their adoption as to encourage others to follow them.

Inverness Advertiser, 1851

SOURCE J

Of the hundreds of Highlanders in and around Dundas at present perhaps not half a dozen understand anything but Gaelic. We may assist these poor creatures for a time, but charity will not keep so many for a very long period. Winter is approaching, and then – but we will leave this painful subject for the present.

Report from a Canadian newspaper, 1851, on the plight of the Highlanders who had gone to Canada

1 *Use the checklists on pages 54 (Master Checklist — Documentary Evidence) and 96 (Checklist — Photographs) to check through these extracts and photographs.*

2 *Describe the feelings, attitudes and concerns of (i) Highlanders who were evicted from their crofts by their landlords and had to decide whether or not to emigrate; (ii) landowners in the Highlands who had to consider reorganising their lands to raise sheep rather than renting to tenants.*

3 *What was it like to live and work on a croft, as in sources A and B?*

4 *Imagine you are the policeman in source G. How do you feel about your part in evicting these Highlanders? Write a conversation between yourself and the tenants you are evicting.*

CAUSE AND EFFECT

Whenever we look at how things change (see pages 116–120), we also look at the causes and consequences (or effects) of making those changes. Scientists in subjects such as physics and chemistry can usually find out for certain why a change occurs. They can repeat an experiment over and over again until they are satisfied with the result. As a result, they know that if they repeat the cause (such as adding sulphuric acid to zinc) they will always get the same result or consequence (zinc sulphate and hydrogen). In history there is no such certainty.

Politicians argue that in appearing to give in to Hitler at Munich in 1938 (see pages 136–138), the British prime minister, Neville Chamberlain, only encouraged the Nazis to invade Poland in 1939. A policy like this, of giving way to a dictator, is called *appeasement*. Munich has since been used as a reason for acting toughly today. In other words, many politicians believe that aggression is the inevitable consequence of a policy of appeasement.

In fact, the Munich Crisis was unique. It is by no means certain that a similar consequence would follow in different circumstances, with another dictator, at another date, in another country. History is not like that. It can show people what happened in the past. It can teach them to learn from their past mistakes. But it cannot lay down strict laws like those you may have learned in science. You can see this illustrated in the cartoon.

THE GAP IN THE BRIDGE

The consequence indicated by this cartoon in *Punch* on 10 December 1919 was the founding of the League of Nations. The cause was the ambition and enthusiasm of the US President, Woodrow Wilson, who wanted to create a common meeting place – the League of Nations – where the countries of the world could settle their disputes peacefully around the conference table instead of on the battlefield. Wilson thought it so important, he insisted that the Treaty of Versailles should include a Covenant setting up the League of Nations. But despite his enthusiasm there was an unpredictable outcome. Many of his fellow Americans favoured a policy of isolationism instead. They did not want the United States to become involved in world problems. On 19 November 1919, the US Senate refused to agree to the terms of the Treaty of Versailles, precisely because it would have meant that the United States would have had to join the League of Nations. The *Punch* cartoonist, like most people in Europe, felt that the world had been let down by the United States. The League – or 'bridge' between nations – had indeed been 'designed by the President of the USA' but the 'keystone' country – the United States – never joined.

Checklist — **Cause and Effect**

Use these checkpoints when you study cause and effect.

1   *What are the suggested effects and consequences?*

2   *Are these effects and consequences facts which can be proved or disproved? Or are they opinions?*

3   *What causes of these effects and consequences have been given?*

4   *Which of these causes can be backed up by facts and evidence? Can they be proved or disproved?*

Going through the Checklist

The following extract is from evidence that Professor Lyon Playfair, a noted British scientist, gave to the Schools Inquiry Commission in 1867. He said that he had asked a number of fellow experts at an industrial exhibition in Paris why there had been a decline in British 'inventiveness and progress in industry' since 1862. This was his summary of their replies.

> The one cause upon which there was most unanimity of conviction is that France, Prussia, Austria, Belgium and Switzerland possess good systems of industrial education for the masters and managers of factories and workshops, and that England has none.

A second cause was also generally, though not so universally, admitted, that we had suffered from the want of cordiality [lack of good feeling] between the employers of labour and workmen, engendered [caused] by the numerous strikes, and more particularly by that rule of many Trades' Unions that men shall work upon an average ability, without giving free scope to the skill and ability which they may individually possess.

1   *What are the suggested effects and consequences?*

Dr Playfair claimed that there had been a decline in British inventiveness and progress in industry between 1862 and 1867.

2   *Are these effects and consequences facts which can be proved or disproved? Or are they opinions?*

They are opinions not facts. It is very difficult indeed to prove a decline in something you cannot actually see, hear or touch! A decline in inventiveness cannot be measured. Nor can a lack of progress in industry. Professor Playfair did not mean a decline in industrial output (which could be measured). He meant a lack of progress in developing new technology.

3   *What causes of these effects and consequences have been given?*

(a)   Lack of effective industrial education in Britain compared with other countries in Europe.

(b)   Lack of co-operation between workers and employers caused by strikes and the insistence of the trade unions on standard rates of pay and standard working conditions.

4   *Which of these causes can be backed up by facts and evidence? Can they be proved or disproved?*

(a)   It was certainly a fact that Britain lacked an effective system of industrial education in the 1860s compared with other countries in Europe. But this does not explain why Britain earlier took the lead in the development of industry, transport and agriculture. There was no lack of inventiveness when the steam engines of Newcomen and Watt were invented; nor at the time of Darby, Cort, Huntsman, Bessemer, Wedgwood, Kay, Hargreaves, Arkwright, Crompton, Cartwright, Brunel, Trevithick, and George and Robert Stephenson.

(b)   The trade unions are often blamed for lack of progress in industry – a matter of opinion rather than a matter of fact. As it happens, one of the most damaging strikes of the 1860s was at Sheffield, where the unions were striking for safer and better working conditions in the cutlery industries. This was hardly a hindrance to progress in industry.

EXERCISES AND ACTIVITIES

The following sources all relate to the dropping of the first atomic bombs on Hiroshima (6 August 1945 – 80 000 people killed) and on Nagasaki (9 August 1945 – 40 000 people killed). Japan surrendered on 15 August 1945.

The atom bomb exploding above Nagasaki on 9 August 1945

SOURCE A

It was hard to believe what we saw . . . We dropped the bomb at exactly 9.15 a.m. and got out of the target area as quickly as possible to avoid the full effect of the explosion. We stayed in the target area two minutes. The smoke rose to a height of 40,000 feet [12,000 metres] . . . We knew at once we had to get the hell out of there. I made a sharp turn in less than half a minute to get broadside to the target. Nothing was visible where only minutes before there was the outline of a city, with its streets and buildings and piers clearly to be seen.

> Colonel Paul Tibbits, captain and pilot of the
> *Enola Gay*, the American Superfortress bomber
> which dropped the first atomic bomb.
> [*Daily Mail*, Wednesday, 8 August 1945]

SOURCE B

AUGUST 8, 1945

Eye-witness accounts of the effect of the first atomic bomb – dropped on Hiroshima, a Japanese city of over 300,000 inhabitants – were received from Guam.

Captain William Parsons of the United States Navy, who observed the attack from the Superfortress which dropped the bomb, said:

'When the bomb fell away, we began putting as much distance between us and the ball of fire which we knew was coming as quickly as possible. There was a terrific flash of light, brilliant as the sun. That was the first indication I had that the bomb worked.'

Each man gasped. What had been Hiroshima was going up in a mountain of smoke.

'First I could see a mushroom of boiling dust apparently with some debris in it up to 20,000 ft. [6,000 metres]. The "boiling" continued for three or four minutes as I watched. Then a white cloud plumed upwards from the centre to some 40,000 ft. [12,000 metres].

An angry dust cloud swirled and spread all round the city. There were fires on the fringes of the city, apparently burning as buildings crumbled and gas mains broke.'

The *Daily Telegraph*, Wednesday, 8 August 1945

SOURCE C

Dr Michihiko Hachiya worked in a hospital in Hiroshima. He described the explosion in his diary on Monday 6 August 1945:

Scorching winds howled around us, whipping dust and ashes into our eyes and up our noses. Our mouths became dry, our throats raw and sore from the biting smoke pulled into our lungs. Coughing was uncontrollable . . .

The streets were deserted except for the dead. Some looked as if they had been frozen by death while in the full action of flight; others lay sprawled as though some giant had flung them from a great height.

Michihiko Hachiya, *Hiroshima Diary*,
translated by Warner Wells

SOURCE D

Ron Bryer, a British prisoner of war, was forced to work in the dockyard at Nagasaki.

He was standing in a small trench in Nagasaki on August 9, 1945, and he watched the atom bomb come down half a mile away . . . We've read all about Schultz and Shevardnadze [the US and Soviet foreign ministers] and their deliberations in Geneva but Bryer knows more about the effects of a nuclear war than the rest of them put together . . .

At about three minutes past the hour [11.03 a.m.], Bryer looked out and saw a large plane flying in over the sea. Suddenly there was a mighty crescendo of noise, like engines over-accelerating. The plane turned and departed, leaving a bomb suspended from three parachutes which drifted slowly down . . .

The violet liquid flash lasted for a long time. There was no explosion – just a series of rocking vibrations. . . . A rushing wind swept debris over him. He blacked out . . . It was pitch black, except for the moving pin-pricks of people on fire. No noise. No screaming. . . . Everything he saw was on silent fire. Telegraph posts burning from the top down, vegetables frying in the fields, and, away down to the left, every ship in the harbour alight . . .

'After what seemed a long, long time, with the sun now up at its high point and all the earth hot and burning, the first real emotion, the first thing I can remember, now slowly coming into my mind, was shame. I started to feel guilty. I looked at my clean hands and felt ashamed.'

Russell Harty in the *Sunday Times*, 29 November 1987

SOURCE E

The atom bomb was no 'great decision' . . . It was merely another powerful weapon in the arsenal of righteousness. The dropping of the bombs stopped the war, saved millions of lives.

President Truman

1   *With each of the five sources A, B, C, D, E, go through the master checklist printed on page 54 and the checklist printed on page 127.*

2   *Are the reported effects and consequences the same in each case? Is the reported cause the same in each case? How do you account for these differences?*

The ruins of the Japanese city of Hiroshima after the dropping of the world's first atom bomb

SELECTING RELEVANT INFORMATION

Selecting relevant information means selecting only those facts, opinions, judgements and ideas which relate specifically to the subject you are studying.

It is interesting to know that Florence Nightingale was called Florence because she was born in Florence in Italy. But this information is irrelevant if you are studying her work as a nurse. It *is* relevant, however, if you are writing the story of her life. It is easy to be side-tracked in this way. This is why you should always try to make an effort to stick to the subject. Only use information which throws light on your topic.

EXERCISES AND ACTIVITIES

The following extract is from a newspaper account of the trial of a young man who had been accused of breaking the new Combination Laws in 1825. These new Combination Laws actually made it easier for trade unions to operate. The old Combination Acts, passed in 1799 and 1800, had effectively banned trade unions since workers could be sent to prison for attending strike meetings or for 'combining' with other workers to force an employer to raise wages or improve working conditions. In this account of the trial of Robert Ford you can find out how the new Combination Laws worked.

Friday, a young man, named Robert Ford, a journeyman shoemaker, was brought up on a warrant charged under the New Act, with endeavouring by threats and intimidation, to prevent one George Turner, from returning to his work.

It appeared that all the men in the employment of Mr Ashenden, a boot and shoemaker, at Hampstead, struck for wages about a fortnight ago. Among the rest were the above-named Ford and Turner. The latter, however, was compelled by the rest to strike against his will; and when the whole party were assembled at a public house debating the matter, he said he was sorry he had left his work, and would return to it; upon which Ford, who was one of the most active promoters of the 'strike' swore, that if he did he would drag him through a pond. This was the 'threat and intimidation' complained of.

Ford, in defence, said he made use of no threat. The words he made use of were these:- 'If you return to your work, you ought to be dragged through a pond.'

Mr Halls [the magistrate] said, Turner had sworn otherwise.

Mr Ashenden said, he should not have brought the prisoner here, but this was not a solitary instance of his having used threats to other men.

Mr Halls said, he certainly should put the act in force against the prisoner. Even now he did it with reluctance, but some check must be put upon the dangerous spirit which seemed to prevail. For the instruction of those whom he saw within hearing he would read that part of one clause of the recent act, which applied to the present case. It stated 'that if any person shall by violence to the person or property, or by threats or intimidation, or by molesting or in any way obstructing another, force or endeavour to force, any journeyman, manufacturer, etc., to depart from his business, or to return his work before it is finished, or preventing any person from returning to his work, etc., every person so offending, or aiding, or assisting therein, shall be imprisoned for any period not exceeding three months'. The act left it to the discretion of the Magistrates whether the hard labour should be added to the imprisonment. The prisoner was sentenced to one month's imprisonment but not to hard labour.

The Age, Sunday, 17 July 1825

1 *Is this a primary source? Is it an eyewitness account? Go through the master checklist on page 143.*

2 *Why was Robert Ford sent to prison? Was it because he went on strike or because he organised the strike? Search through this passage and find the relevant part of the evidence and the relevant part of the Combination Laws which sent him to prison for one month.*

3 *Which of the following did the new Combination Laws prohibit:*
   (a) going on strike
   (b) standing in the path of someone wishing to return to work
   (c) threatening a fellow worker
   (d) peaceful picketing (i.e. asking fellow workers not to go back to work)
   (e) erecting a barrier across the entrance to the works to stop people returning to work?

FOR AND AGAINST

A *reasoned argument* is one in which each stage of the argument follows from the preceding one. It uses good reasons to argue the case for or against. The reasons are good because they are based on known facts rather than on bias, prejudice or inaccurate facts. Use this checklist when you examine the arguments in any historical source.

Checklist — A Reasoned Argument

1 *List the arguments for.*

2 *List the arguments against.*

3 *Which of these arguments are based on facts and which are opinions? Which can be proved? Which are unprovable?*

4 *Which arguments seem to you to be backed up by the most convincing evidence? Which arguments are weak and unconvincing? Which side has the better case?*

Going through the Checklist

The extracts that follow are from an article by Frederick Ryland in *The Girl's Own Paper*, in 1896, discussing the arguments for and against votes for women. This was several years before the founding of the suffragette movement.

EXTRACT A

Men and women certainly do not entirely understand each other's point of view, and there are many questions, some great and some small, in which women as a rule take a line of their own.

EXTRACT B

Then there is the argument for justice. Why should a person otherwise qualified be refused a vote simply on the ground of sex? Mr A. at No. 1 has a vote; Mrs B at No. 2, with equal education, and an equal stake in the country, is refused a vote, merely because she is a woman. This seems on the face of it to be an outrage on fairness. But, as a matter of fact, things are usually worse, since Mrs B's gardener or coachman will probably have a vote, while she is without one.

EXTRACT C

Suppose, for instance, the vast majority of men were in favour of a war with Russia, and the women vetoed it, or vice versa; in either case it would be felt that as the men supply by far the greater part of the blood and the treasure which would be spent on a war, and are out of all comparison in a better position to judge of the effect of such a war on the honour, welfare, and commerce of the country, with them must rest the final decision.

Frederick Ryland, 'Politics for Girls: Female Suffrage', *The Girl's Own Paper*, 16 May 1896

1   *List the arguments* for.

(a) Women have their own opinions and these should be heard.
(b) It is unfair to give the vote to men and not to women with the same qualifications.

2   *List the arguments* against.

(c) Women should not be able to vote on issues which might result in a war which men would have to fight and finance.
(d) Men are better able to judge the effect of such a war on the country.

3   *Which of these arguments are based on facts and which are opinions? Which can be proved? Which are unprovable?*

Arguments (a), (b) and (c) are based on provable facts – (a) women do have their own opinions, (b) some women in 1896 did have the same voting qualifications as men, (c) in 1896 men fought wars not women [but note that women directly and indirectly helped to finance them]. Argument (d) is Frederick Ryland's unprovable opinion.

4 *Which arguments seem to you to be backed up by the most convincing evidence? Which arguments are weak and unconvincing? Which side has the better case?*

Arguments (a) and (b) are backed by convincing evidence. There is no logical answer to either argument.

Argument (c) is arrogant nonsense. As Ryland knew, 'by far the greater part of the blood' spent on a war in 1896 would have been given *not* by men entitled to vote *but* by young men under 21 who were unable to vote, and by other young men over 21 who were disqualified from voting because they were not householders. Argument (d), that men can better judge the effect of a war, is rubbish if the insane celebrations in August 1914 are any guide (see pages 110–112).

Lady Dorothy Howard arguing the cause of the suffragettes at a political meeting in 1908

EXERCISES AND ACTIVITIES

The brief extracts that follow are just some of the many different opinions which were expressed in the two or three days immediately following the signing of the Munich Peace Agreement on 30 September 1938.

1   *Examine the arguments carefully and then list them in two columns – the arguments for and the arguments against.*

2   *Which of the arguments used by the supporters and opponents of the Munich Agreement are based on facts and which are opinions? Which arguments do you think could be supported by proof? Which are unprovable?*

3   *Which arguments seem to you to be backed up by the most convincing evidence? Which arguments are weak and unconvincing? Which side has the better case?*

4   *How would you have reacted to the Munich Agreement on 1 October 1938?*

Londoners digging trenches in preparation for war – September 1938

SOURCE A   ... the settlement is only putting off the evil day ...

Letter in *Daily Herald*

SOURCE B   Who'll trust us? It's like throwing your own kid to the wolves. We helped make it a country and then Chamberlain comes along and wants to buy that swine off. There'll be a war sooner or later, then there'll be nobody to help us.

London bus conductor

SOURCE C

So it is peace, and a Chamberlain, respectable gentleman's peace: the whole world rejoices whilst only a few malcontents jeer.

Sir Henry Channon – a Conservative MP

SOURCE D

... the German dictator, instead of snatching his victuals from the table, has been content to have them served to him course by course ... we have sustained a defeat without a war

Winston Churchill – a Conservative MP

SOURCE E

The peace of Munich has left us less strong than we were yesterday, since we have lost an ally, and more than 30 German divisions will be available to be turned against us. If we were incapable of resisting the formidable German menace in the past when we were stronger, how will we resist the next time when we will be less strong?

French newspaper – *L'Epoque*

SOURCE F

They [the Germans] are being enriched by a territory [the Czechoslovak Sudetenland] abundantly provided and marvel-lously equipped.

French newspaper – *Le Figaro*

SOURCE G

The Munich agreement has done better than put aside war. It has brought back into the hearts of all the love of peace and has shown in a striking fashion that the most difficult problems can henceforward be resolved round a table.

French newspaper – *L'Oeuvre*

SOURCE H

Let no man say too high a price has been paid for peace in Europe until he has searched his soul and found himself willing to risk in war the lives of those who are nearest and dearest to him.

New York Times

SOURCE I

There is little now to prevent Hitler from dominating and organising Middle and Eastern Europe.

Chicago Tribune

SOURCE J

The Nobel Prize should be awarded to Mr. Chamberlain. The whole world agrees that nobody ever did more for peace. The prize was created for men like him.

Norwegian newspaper – *Tidens Tegn*

SOURCE K

Britain and France have consented under a threat of war to give Germany control of important and strategic industrial areas.

Sydney Morning Herald

SOURCE L

Mr. Chamberlain's great victory is that he won the fight for a civilised system of settling big issues around the council table and not on the battlefield.

Montreal Star

SOURCE M

The Prime Minister has confidence in the good will and in the word of Herr Hitler, although when Herr Hitler broke the Treaty of Versailles he undertook to keep the Treaty of Locarno, and when he broke the Treaty of Locarno he undertook not to have further territorial aims in Europe. When he entered Austria he authorized his henchmen to give an authoritative assurance that he would not interfere with Czechoslovakia, and that was less than six months ago.

Duff Cooper – a Government Minister who resigned from the Cabinet in protest at the signing of the Munich Agreement

SOURCE N

He [Hitler] has successfully divided and reduced to impotence the forces which might have stood against the rule of violence . . . Today we are in a dangerous position. We are left isolated. All potential allies have gone . . .

Clement Attlee [Labour Party] – Leader of the Opposition

SOURCE O

Owing to her geographical position, if war had come, whoever won or lost, Czechoslovakia would have been inevitably destroyed with immense slaughter and devastation.

Sir Samuel Hoare – Home Secretary

SOURCE P

. . . there were, he maintained four hopeful features. For the first time a dictator had made some concession. Again, dictators had learned that hatred of war prevailed among their own well-drilled peoples. . . . Thirdly, in spite of Dr. Goebbels, the German people now knew that Britain too wanted peace; and lastly, there was a great awakening in this country to the need that conciliation must be backed by strength [i.e. rearmament].

Report of speech by Sir John Simon – Chancellor of the Exchequer

REACHING A CONCLUSION

In an examination, or in a special study, you will often have to reach a conclusion. This is a summing up of what you know about a topic. A good conclusion will balance different opinions and arguments against each other and then state clearly the verdict of the writer. A good conclusion will also be supported by facts and historical evidence (if this is available). But it will avoid making generalisations based on only one or two examples.

In the extract printed opposite you can read about the visit made by a woman writer to two cotton mills near Bolton in about 1844. These were the only factories she saw but she used them to make this generalisation: 'The factory people are better clothed, better fed, and better conducted than many other classes of working-people.' This conclusion is the exact opposite of the one reached by Lord Ashley (later Earl Shaftesbury) and by other people who tried to improve working conditions in textile mills and coal mines in the early nineteenth century. They knew that some factories were well run, like those of Robert Owen at his mills in New Lanark in Scotland. But the appalling working conditions in many mills, factories, and mines were recorded in writing by hundreds of eyewitnesses. Their evidence reveals:

- dangerous machines left unguarded so that accidents were common
- young children employed to crawl under machines to do dangerous jobs
- women and children doing back-breaking jobs
- employees working very long hours
- tired children making mistakes and causing serious accidents
- children often being beaten when they were tired or when they made mistakes
- air filled with dust so that workers breathed it into their lungs, causing diseases
- a deafening clatter from looms and from other machines
- suffocatingly hot and humid air in summer
- cold and badly-heated factories in winter
- poorly ventilated mines, mills and factories
- gloomy and badly lit workplaces
- dirty buildings often infested with vermin and polluted by waste
- overworked, underfed, and underpaid workers.

The agitation to improve working conditions made some progress with the passing of the Factory Act in 1844. This limited the legal hours of work in textile mills for all women, girls and boys under 18 years. Children under 13 years could only work in a mill on a 'half-time' basis. The Act also demanded that dangerous machines be screened to make them safe to use.

EXERCISES AND ACTIVITIES

Sixteen days after the passing of the Factory Act, *Chambers's Journal* printed this account of a visit to two cotton mills at Turton and Egerton (near Bolton in Lancashire).

I found the mill a large building, with a wide stone staircase, easy of ascent and very clean. The working rooms are spacious, well-ventilated, and lofty, kept at an equable temperature, and, like all parts of the factory, exceedingly clean. There are a number of windows in each room, indeed so many, that I wondered if they had any window-duty to pay ...

I observed that great care had been bestowed upon the 'boxing-up' of dangerous machinery, and was told that accidents were very rare, and that when they did occur, they were the 'result of the greatest stupidity or negligence'.

After examining everything, I came to the conclusion that the nature of factory labour would have no deteriorating effect on those engaged in it; in which opinion I was confirmed by seeing the healthy appearance of the operatives about me. Many girls who were at work – I may say all, for I saw no exceptions – looked healthy and happy. Their ages, I should think, varied from fourteen to four-and-twenty ...

If an operative has a number of children, he generally endeavours to procure employment for them at the mill where he works, and their united earnings make them very comfortable ...

Now that I have seen the factory people at their work, in their cottages, and in their schools, I am totally at a loss to account for the outcry that has been made against them ...

The millowners, as far as I can judge, are most anxious to contribute to their happiness and welfare, and the operatives themselves seem quite contented with their situation. With respect to infant, or more properly, juvenile labour, I do not see how it can be dispensed with ...

My opinion is, that as long as the masses have to earn their bread by the sweat of their brows, we cannot expect to see them better off, more comfortable, or more happy than the factory operatives of the north of England.

Anonymous woman writer, *Chambers's Journal*,
22 June 1844

Inside a cotton textile mill in about 1840

1   *Go through the master checklist on page 143.*

2   *How many cotton mills did she visit? How far apart were they? Did she see a fair selection of mills from all over northern England?*

3   *What did she base her conclusions on – facts or opinions?*

4   *What were her conclusions? Make a list of them. Then take each conclusion, point by point and write a short criticism of it.*

5   *Which of the list of complaints printed on page 139 does the writer appear to contradict? Do you think she went out of her way to look for 'evidence' which put the employer in a favourable light?*

6   *After reading this extract there are a number of possible conclusions we might come to. Here are just a few. See if you can add to them.*
    ● *That conditions were excellent in all cotton textile mills in 1844 (as the writer implies in her article).*
    ● *That conditions were excellent in some cotton textile mills in 1844.*
    ● *That the visitor was extremely lucky to visit two rare examples of well-managed textile mills.*
    ● *That the visitor was hoodwinked by the owners and by the managers in the two mills she visited.*
    ● *That the visitor was biased and could have had a financial interest in these or other cotton mills.*
    ● *That the visitor was lying and hoodwinked the editor of the magazine which printed her article.*
    Which seems to you to be the most sensible balanced conclusion on the basis of all the facts and evidence provided in the article?

7   *Does your conclusion agree with all the facts? If not, why not? Which evidence points to some conclusion other than the one you have reached?*

Summary Checklists

Master Checklist — Documentary Evidence

1 What does the source tell you about the past?

2 What is the origin of the source? What type of evidence is it (e.g. diary, letter, newspaper report)? Is it likely to be reliable?

3 Why was the source written? Was it written to justify the writer's actions? Does the writer try to take credit for successes which other people claim for themselves? Does the writer put the blame for failures on to other people?

4 When was the source written? Is it a primary source, dating from the time of the event which it describes? Or is it a secondary source?

5 Is there any clue or statement to show that it is an actual eyewitness account? Was the writer in a good position to say what happened? Does the source agree with other eyewitness accounts of the same event? Are there any reasons for thinking the eyewitness cannot be trusted entirely?

6 If the source was written years after the event, is there any reason to doubt the accuracy of the writer's memory?

7 Which parts of the extract seem to you to be opinions, and not facts which can be proved right or wrong? Are the opinions based on facts or on prejudice? Has the writer used words of approval or disapproval, or colourful or exaggerated phrases, to try to influence the reader?

8 Does the author show any other signs of bias or prejudice? Does the writer appear to take sides in an argument?

9 Are there any obvious mistakes or errors of fact in the extract? Which statements are supported by facts you know about from other sources? Does anything in the extract contradict other sources, or facts which you already know to be true?

10 Does the account give a distorted view of events which actually occurred? Has the author left out facts which tell a different story? Is any part of the extract an obvious lie or exaggeration? Are there any obvious gaps in the evidence, such as missing dates, facts, or personalities?

Checklist — Pictures from the Past

1 Does the picture attempt realistically to portray people, events, buildings, etc., or does it poke fun at them by means of a cartoon or an exaggerated drawing (called a caricature)?

2 What does the picture show? What does it tell us about the past?

3 When was the picture drawn? Was it drawn at roughly the same time as the event or feature it depicts? Is it a primary source? If no date is given can you estimate roughly the date when it was drawn from the clothes worn by the people in the picture, from styles of vehicle (such as motor cars), or from other clues?

4 Why was the picture drawn or painted? Was it simply an illustration (e.g. to accompany a news item or to illustrate a book), or is there any reason to think the artist was using the picture to make you feel in a certain way about the events or people depicted? For instance, was it drawn or painted to make you want to protest against an injustice, or to feel excited, or sad, or nostalgic for an old way of life, or patriotic, or self-satisfied, or envious of someone else's way of life?

5 Does the picture show something which could not be shown in any other way, such as the interior of a courtroom where photographs are not permitted?

6 Even if it looks like a realistic picture, is there any reason to think it is a product of the artist's imagination rather than a portrayal of an actual scene or event?

7 If the picture is a cartoon, what was the artist getting at? What does the cartoon tell you about the topic, events or people portrayed? What does it tell you about the attitude of the artist who drew the cartoon or of the magazine which published it?

Checklist — Photographs

1 What does the photograph show? What does it tell us about the past?

2 When and where was the photograph taken? If no date is given, use clues to estimate the date.

3 Why was the photograph taken? Is there any reason to think the photographer chose a viewpoint or a subject to make us feel in a certain way about the event or people depicted?

4   *Is there any sign that the people in the photograph are posing for the photographer? Were they aware of the camera? Does this make any difference to the value of the photograph?*

5   *Is there any reason to think that the photograph is not a typical example of what it appears to show? Is there any reason to think that it may have been altered in any way?*

Checklist — **Relics from the Past**

1   *What was the purpose of the tool, machine, vehicle, or building you are studying? What was it used for? Why was it built or made?*

2   *Can you date the object or building either exactly or approximately?*

3   *Where is it situated now or where was it found? Where did it come from originally?*

4   *What does it tell us about people in the past?*

Checklist — **Maps and Plans**

1   *When was the map drawn? What does it show? If it is a special map why was it drawn?*

2   *Is the map accurately drawn? Has it got a scale? If not, work out the scale for yourself. Compare measurements on the old map between three landmarks (e.g. churches) and then compare them with the same measurements on a modern map. In this way you can tell if the map was drawn roughly to scale or not (since the three landmarks will not have moved their position since the date when the old map was drawn).*

3   *What is the particular value of the map (if any) as a source of historical information?*

Checklist — **Statistics**

1   When and how were the statistics collected? Who collected them? Were they in a position to collect accurate or reliable statistics? Can we be certain they are not guesses, estimates, approximations, or even lies?

2   Is it likely that someone else working in exactly the same way would collect the same statistics? If not, why not?

3   Are the statistics complete or only a sample of all the possible statistics which could have been recorded?

4   Who selected the statistics for use and how were they chosen?

5   What do the statistics tell you about the past? What do they prove? If they are quoted to back up a statement, do they really support the conclusions drawn from them by the writer?

6   Are the statistics used to support a statement which may be biased or prejudiced?

7   If averages are used, do they mean anything? See if you can find out how they were calculated.

Checklist — **Change**

1   What was the nature of the change? Was it part of a much bigger change?

2   Was it an important and significant change? Did it affect everybody and almost every activity, like the coming of the railway, motor car and telephone? Or did it affect just a section of the community, such as the effect of the means test in the 1930s on the unemployed?

3   Who or what benefited from the change? Who or what suffered from the change?

4   Did the change take place suddenly, rapidly, steadily, slowly, jerkily, or imperceptibly?

5   Did the change affect people mainly because of its political effects, such as its effect on relations with other countries? Or because of its social and economic effects, such as on health or on industry?

Checklist — Cause and Effect

1   *What are the suggested effects and consequences?*

2   *Are these effects and consequences facts which can be proved or disproved? Or are they opinions? For instance, the statement that 'the population of London trebled in size between 1851 and 1931' is a consequence which can be easily proved if you look at the census statistics. But the statement that 'young people were better behaved fifty years ago' is an opinion. It cannot be proved or disproved to everyone's satisfaction.*

3   *What causes of these effects and consequences have been given?*

4   *Which of these causes can be backed up by facts and evidence? Can they be proved or disproved?*

Checklist — A Reasoned Argument

1   *List the arguments* for.

2   *List the arguments* against.

3   *Which of these arguments are based on facts and which are opinions? Which can be proved? Which are unprovable?*

4   *Which arguments seem to you to be backed up by the most convincing evidence? Which arguments are weak and unconvincing? Which side has the better case?*

Checklist — The Link with the Past

1   *Find out if there are any features, such as buildings, monuments, street names, or house names near your home which link up in some way with the topic.*

2   *Which of your living relatives (if any) were alive for part of the time covered by the topic? What do they remember about this period?*

3   *What things from the past can you find in your local museum or library which link up with this topic?*

Index

CONCEPTS, SKILLS AND SOURCES

THEMES IN STANDARD GRADE HISTORY